247 Days

Father Dan Kennedy
A Proud and Happy Priest

Daniel J. Kennedy, Sr.

DEDICATION

To Alice, and to all women
blessed to be the mothers of priests.

Contents

DEDICATION 5

INTRODUCTION 9

PROLOGUE 13

PART ONE: DANNY BOY 15

Chapter 1: Our Awesome God 17

Chapter 2: "It's a Boy?" 38

Chapter 3: Knights of the Round Table 63

PART TWO: DAN THE MAN 73

Chapter 4: Home Away From Home 75

Chapter 5: Like Mother, Like Son 86

Chapter 6: "Call Waiting!" 95

Chapter 7: Embarking on Seminary Life 112

Chapter 8: Scituate Harbor 135

Chapter 9: Leave of Absence 156

PART THREE: FATHER DAN 187

Chapter 11: Rite of Ordination 189

Chapter 12: Rookie Priest; Apprentice Parish Priest 206

Chapter 13: Minister of the Sacraments 226

Chapter 14: Advent at Sea, Christmas at Home 241

Chapter 15: Same Skyline; Different Angle 251

Chapter 16: We Need Men Who Think Like You 261

APPENDIX 267

ACKNOWLEDGEMENTS 285

INTRODUCTION

He who has ears to hear, let him hear. (Mark 4:9)

Father Daniel J. Kennedy had hundreds of friends and they already know much of this story — the winding course that took him across several continents, through nine marathons, in and out of the seminary, and finally to ordination as a Catholic priest. Father Dan's style was to go at a 24/7 pace and, as a newly ordained priest, he kept up that pace. Day or night he answered calls with a cheerful grin and genuine concern, but after just eight months after receiving Holy Orders — 247 days — Father Dan was called to his eternal home, when an undetected heart condition felled him just eleven days after his 34th birthday.

I decided to write this story of Danny's dogged run toward his vocation in the hope that it will move other young man to focus on their purpose on this earth. I pray they will say, just as Father Dan said, *"Here I am, Lord. Did you call?"* I would like them to pray and to ponder what their Creator desires for them. As Father Jim DiPerri said, "Dan had a deep understanding of the Real Presence of Christ and he possessed the desire to grow in his love for the Lord and for His people".

Yes, my son Danny's story is uniquely his own, but yearning to know God's will is the desire of every heart. That former party animal St. Augustine figured it out around A.D. 400: *"You have made us for yourself, O Lord, and our heart is restless until it rests in you."*

This is the story of the Lord's persistence in guiding a stubborn young man who was fully engaged with life to turn his long stride toward priesthood. As a college student he entertained the vision of himself as a priest of Christ, but the image faded when he was swept up in the world of work, travel, and play. Yet he remained a faithful Catholic, and he never stopped wondering what God really wanted from him.

When Danny entered the seminary he was 27 years old and still uncertain whether he had a priestly vocation. Indeed, halfway through the program in order to clear his mind he took a leave of absence. After a short leave, fully convinced he was following the will of the Lord, he returned to St. John's Seminary and, at age 33 was ordained to Christ's Holy Priesthood.

My view as his father was intimate yet limited, so I called on many of his friends and colleagues to share their insights to round out this story. I am grateful for their help in describing the shy little boy who grew into a confident man, comfortable in any situation, from tailgaters to teaching. He had sharp elbows in a hockey game as well as a sharp wit combined with boundless energy and abundant kindness for everyone.

Danny's friends need no memoir to recall; his flashing smile, tremendous energy, and genuine interest in everyone he met. My purpose in documenting his life is not merely to describe my son. This is an attempt to demonstrate that the Lord never ceases to draw people to Himself and, he will never stop drawing men to His Holy Priesthood.

Many have asked and still ask: "Why was this joyful young priest granted such a short period of service?" Yes, a penetrating question!

Danny prided himself in giving a firm handshake. Perhaps the answer to this question lies in Francis Thompson's poem, "The Hound of Heaven," with Christ's pursuit of the fleeing soul, who, at last, hears the happiest words of all: "Rise, clasp My hand, and come!" God's time is not ours, and though we count 247 days as short it was sufficient for Christ to teach my son — and all who knew him — a lesson of joyful, hopeful, and faithful surrender to God's will. Deo gratias.

Daniel J. Kennedy, Sr.

August 22, 2015

Notes:

All net proceeds from this book will be donated to the Father Daniel J. Kennedy Memorial Scholarship Fund at Saint John's Seminary in Brighton, MA.

Additional photos, multimedia and links are available on the book's website: www.247days.org.

All In God's Providence: Danny died on 1/27 after having been formed for the priesthood at 127 Lake Street (St. John's Seminary). Danny died exactly one year after his ordination to the clergy as a transitional deacon. Danny's priestly ministry lasted 247 days, with Danny giving 24/7 energy each of those days.

PROLOGUE

Almost two hundred years ago, a Dominican priest, Fr. Jean-Baptiste Henri Lacordaire, O.P. poignantly captured the essence of the priesthood in his prayer, "Thou Art a Priest Forever":

"To live in the midst of the world with no desire for its pleasures; to be a member of every family, yet belonging to none; to share all sufferings; to heal all wounds; to daily go from men to God to offer Him their homage and petitions; to return from God to men to bring them His pardon and hope; to bless and to be blest forever. O God, what a life, and it is yours, O Priest of Jesus Christ."

PART ONE: DANNY BOY

Chapter 1: Our Awesome God

The Lord gave and the Lord has taken away; blessed be the name of the Lord. (Job 1:21b)

January in Massachusetts is not for the faint of heart, yet Alice who is stout of heart opted not to accompany me to Cape Cod on Sunday afternoon to fulfill a family errand. Even though the roads were dry in Needham and, after countless summer trips with our five children the drive was routine, driving in winter weather was unappealing to Alice.

Today's mission was simple: fetch home our granddaughter Ashley, who had been visiting her mother Patti at the Cape. Patti was the second of our five children (Katie, Patti, Anne Marie, Danny and Jack). The farther I drove the darker the sky became, and, as I crossed the Sagamore Bridge a heavy snowfall began to cover the road. At the appropriated point of rendezvous we met up with Patti and Ashley, safely secured Ashley in the back seat and bid Patti a hurried farewell. Amid the driving snow I carefully reversed course, relieved to be heading home to Needham. Mission nearly accomplished!

En route my cell phone, which was wired to ring through the car radio speaker system, rang. Ashley and I were stunned when we heard Patti's quivering voice. She was obviously trembling. Patti frantically explained that she encountered an icy patch on Route 6; her car spun out, careened into a ditch and smashed into a tree. She explained, in order to exit the car, she had to crawl through the shattered windshield. She also assured us that she was not injured and that it was pointless for us to turn back as the police and a tow truck were already on the scene. Then she added; "I don't know why God allowed me to live." "Deo gratias," I murmured.

Then my thoughts turned toward another child of ours who was also on the road that day, our son Danny. Father Dan had driven three hours from Boston to Fairfield, Connecticut to baptize a new-born baby of a close friend. I knew he intended to drive the coastal route on his return trip back to Boston so I decided to acquaint him with the hazardous road conditions. When I spoke with him and informed him of Patti's accident I suggested that he return via an inland route to avoiding the coastal storm, he quickly agreed with me — unusually, for a guy noted for his stubbornness.

There was an ancillary benefit as well; an inland route would allow him to visit two newlyweds in Simsbury, Connecticut whom he had married the past October: our son Jack and his bride Beth. Both of our extremely competitive sons had long since outgrown their childhood tussles epitomizing true 'brotherly love' for each other. The route revision would allow them an opportunity to hang out together and hoist a brew.

As I sat in front of the television, preparing to watch the 11:00 o'clock news, I mulled over the crisis of the day, Patti's near cata-strophic accident, when the telephone rang. I muttered; "Who's violating Kennedy family rules at this hour?" All five children and their friends have known for years that no calls were welcome at the Kennedy residence after 9:30 at night. What nonsensical child-ish chatter could matter more than bedtime quiet? The only ex-ception to our ironclad family rule was a family emergency.

The phone call was from Jack's wife Beth calling us with terrible news. "Can you come, right now?" she begged. Danny had sud-denly collapsed in their living room, and an ambulance was rushing him to St. Francis Hospital in Hartford, Connecticut. Jack was in the ambulance with Danny. I raced upstairs to wake Alice and inform her of this terrible news. I will not forget the bewildered expression on her face as I explained the urgency of the situation. Within a minute or two we were in the car, the second 'family mission' of the day, this time an incomprehensible mission!

Shortly after we passed through the tollbooth on the Massachusetts Turnpike my phone rang, it was Jack. Both of us gasped as we heard Jack's broken voice; "Mom, Dad" — then tears. In a moment he collected himself enough to say that he had pleaded with God, but the doctors could not revive Danny. His brother, our son, one of Boston's recently ordained priests, had died. We listened intently as Jack started to recount what had so shockingly transpired. Alice and I were too stunned to speak or to even cry.

Surely, if anyone was indestructible it was our Danny. One week earlier he turned 34 and commenced his annual training program for his tenth marathon. Just two months ago he had passed the United States Navy Physical Examination pursuant to serving as Navy Chaplain on board the USS Nimitz CVN-68 during deployment in the Pacific Ocean. It was impossible to comprehend the reason such a high-energy athlete, in superior physical condition, would die so suddenly, in the prime of life.

Through his tears, Jack struggled to describe their last hour together, when Danny had been telling stories of his first assignment as a new priest and his excitement at starting his second assignment within a few days. "Dad, he was so, so, happy!" Jackie kept repeating. "I never saw him any happier."

Danny told Jack and Beth the thrill of celebrating his final parish Mass that morning at St. John the Evangelist in Winthrop, MA. He was moved when parishioners of all ages crowded the farewell reception at the parish center, full of thanks and compliments. The

Winthrop Catholic Women's Club had baked, CCD students decorated the hall and the youngsters posted placards on the walls of the auditorium reading: Good Bye, Fr. Dan, Thank you Fr. Dan, Come back to see us Fr. Dan, etc. Danny hadn't realized how many lives he had touched in the eight months he served in Winthrop.

Immediately after departing the parish reception Fr. Dan jumped into his car for a three-hour drive to Fairfield, Connecticut to baptize Kelly Elizabeth Blute at St. Thomas Aquinas Church in Fairfield, CT, the newborn daughter of two close friends. "It was a privilege to baptize that little baby girl," he told Jack hours afterward. "I'm so happy to be a priest!" Only a few minutes later, to Jack's horror, Danny collapsed and slumped down in the chair.

As Alice and I continued to process this truly, unbelievable news, Jack advised us to return home and not travel on to Connecticut. At the first opportunity I pulled the car off the Massachusetts Turnpike at the Charlton Rest Stop in order to try and process a myriad of thoughts that were swirling through our heads. As Alice and I exited the car, we hugged and cried. After a few minutes we went into the Coffee Shop turned around without coffee and wandered back to our car. Tears flowed freely down our faces; inexplicable thoughts crossed our minds and incomprehensible words emanated from our mouths.

Although I don't think I realize it at the time, I subsequently recalled stopping at the Coffee Shop at the Charlton Rest Stop in March of 1982. I was in-route to Springfield to attend the funeral of Bishop Christopher J. Weldon and met Humberto Cardinal Medeiros who was also in route to Springfield to celebrate Bishop Weldon's Funeral Mass.

As Alice and I stood hugging each other, debilitated from such shocking news, I thought it interesting that Danny's last ministerial act was to welcome a baby girl into the Catholic Church at St. Thomas the Aquinas Church in Fairfield, CT because it was at St. Thomas Aquinas Friary at Providence College that his 'path to priesthood' began to crystalize.

Neither Alice nor I could rationalize any logical explanation of what happened. We were content to continue hugging each other and quietly weep under what was an amazingly glorious moonlit sky, replete with millions of extraordinarily bright stars.

When Danny was seven years old on East Mountain Road in Westfield, he looked up at these stars and wondered aloud, "what is God doing tonight?" and, just six weeks ago, as a lieutenant in the United States Navy he again gazed in awe at these same brilliant stars high above the dark Pacific Ocean while on board the USS Nimitz. In his Christmas Eve homily, Father Dan compared the radiance of the stars over the Pacific Ocean to what must have been the brilliance of the Star of Bethlehem. He proceeded to link the stars over the Pacific Ocean with the Star of Bethlehem, the Light of Christ, which, as he said, overcomes any type of darkness that may enter our lives.

As Alice and I continued to be transfixed by the brilliance of the stars which illuminated the Rest Stop and the Massachusetts Turnpike, I thought Danny must be somewhere amongst those stars. In my imagination, I could visualize Danny striding, with his usual rapid gait, in search of the Lord. Surely, on seeing him approach, Jesus would smile and turn to His Father and say, "Here comes Danny Kennedy; he's a friend of mine!"

Danny entered Eternal Life on January 27, 2008, the monthly octave of his First Mass of Thanksgiving on Pentecost Sunday, May 27, 2007. Only eight months as a priest; yet in the days and weeks and years to come we would hear story after story of how his gift of priesthood, his joy for life, and his love for Christ had inspired countless people in those 247 days. I know Father Dan's legacy is still unfolding, as his brother seminarians — now priests themselves — share the story of this stubborn man's desire to follow God's will, which led him to the Altar, smiling and laughing, as he triumphantly crossed the finish line.

A Week of Wakes

A time to weep, and a time to laugh.
(Ecclesiastes 3:4a)

When Alice and I returned home it was after Midnight. We were surprised to see that lights were on in every room of the house; it reminded us of Christmas Eve. Our daughter Katie had called family and friends; all night long people arrived. At first we could only sit in stunned silence. Two of Danny's most upbeat pals, Father Matt Westcott and Father Patrick Armano, embraced Alice and me with tears filling their eyes. Eventually Father Patrick managed some consoling words, but Father Matt, customarily gregarious, just sat in his favorite chair stunned, completely shocked with the unfathomable news. Katie, our daughter Anne Marie, our granddaughter Ashley, and Anne Marie's friend Dave Russell, joined us at 45 Woodlawn Ave. Jackie remained at St. Francis Hospital in Hartford and Patti recuperated from her accident on the Cape.

As the night wore on the atmosphere changed, swinging back and forth from sad regret to comical reminiscence, then from tears to laughter and laughter to tears. The impromptu gathering had become the Kennedy Family's version of a traditional Irish Wake; laughter and stories amidst tears of sorrow. Three days prior Father Dan used our marble-topped table to celebrate a family Mass in memory of Alice's departed cousin. Now that same table was piled high with food and drink in honor of Danny's own departure.

In spite of such an unexpected and truly devastating occurrence almost immediately, our entire family, Alice and I, our four children, and granddaughter seemed to be consoled and comforted as we attempted to digest what had happened. From a human standpoint, we were of course deeply saddened and extremely confused, yet from a spiritual standpoint we were calm and composed. God instilled inner strength in both of us. We accepted this challenge with the utmost confidence that this was indeed, God's will. God's Presence to us at that time was definitely apparent in helping us cope. God's Presence to our entire family was truly, awesome. Never, were any of us remonstrative or recriminatory!

Not my will but yours be done.
(Luke 22:42)

After everyone had departed, around 4:00am on 28th of January, Alice and I locked the front door, stood in the front hallway and hugged each other. Suddenly, through remnants of a tear stained face, Alice said to me; "Just think, just think" as she most assuredly stated; "he is with the Blessed Mother". As proliferous tears continued to flow down her reddened cheeks, she repeated with the utmost confidence and joy, "He - is with the Blessed Mother!"

Deep is the wisdom of the maternal heart.

Among all the comforting words exchanged during that long night, to my knowledge, no one had mentioned the Blessed Mother until that moment. Apparently Alice could empathize with Mary as she too lost a priest-son at a comparable age.

As Alice and I retired for what remained of the evening, sleep eluded me. After tossing and turning, I finally decided to maintain my daily schedule and attend the 6:50 a.m. Mass at our Needham parish, St. Joseph. I knew that I was scheduled to be the Altar Server and I intended to fulfill that commitment. Additionally, I thought maintaining my daily routine would help me stay on track at least that is what I told myself. Actually, in times of duress, being close to the Eucharist has always been a source of comfort.

When I arrived in the Sacristy my face must have revealed the stress of the past 12 hours, as others in the Sacristy urged me to step aside and take a pew. I concurred. Nonetheless, for the rest of the week I insisted on keeping to the schedule and serving the 6:50 a.m. Mass. Subsequently several of the daily communicants told me that my presence on the Altar during that difficult week strengthened them.

Every morning, after the 6:50 Mass, I stopped at Dunkin' Donuts for several "Boxes o' Joe" to fortify the non-stop stream of visitors who were showing up at our house with bagels, muffins, coffeecakes, donuts, and pies. People are so good, so kind and so generous during a crisis. There were self-organized; cooking crews, cleaning crews, even house sitters when we had to go out. Neighbors and friends staffed our kitchen, organizing an abundance of food; complete dinners of turkey, ham, roast beef, chicken pies, plus endless desserts. Alice said we could have fed the entire crew of the USS Nimitz. In the end, the Needham Community Center was a beneficiary, as even with a full house we could not possibly consume all the food.

Every day priests, seminarians, friends, relatives, school chums, and neighbors came with some version of the expected Irish words of condolence, "I'm sorry for your loss." Yet their grieving was laced with gaiety — a classic Irish wake. Danny's quips and practical jokes were recounted left and right. He did have a wonderful sense of humor.

Remember when, he sneaked in and rang the seminary bell after the Red Sox won the World Series in 2004?

Remember after walking up four flights of stairs to pick-up Cardinal Seán O'Malley's suitcase he teased him about not having an episcopal elevator?

Remember when, he filled the front lawn on Woodlawn Ave with Budweiser inflatables and Mr. Kennedy blew his stack? Or when he hit that long drive into a brook and, barefoot, with his pants rolled-up he blasted the ball out of the water and proceeded to cover himself with muddy water?

Remember the time when a seminarian was sick and Danny secured a commode and placed the commode along with several rolls of toilet paper, an empty pail along with a sympathy card signed by brother seminarians and, the Boston Herald outside his door?

Remember...remember?

Alice and I were especially moved by the arrival of Danny's good friend Patrick Murphy with his wife Cristina. Patrick had driven from Boston to Hartford at midnight to be with Jackie at St. Francis Hospital in Hartford as he sat next to Danny all night.

Gently Patrick asked me, "Do you remember the night my father died?" Bereft, Patrick had come over to our house to be with his pals, Danny and Jackie. "Patrick," Danny told him that night, "in spite of how much your father loved your mother and your sisters and you, if he could come back he wouldn't!" Danny explained how he saw it: "Your father lived his entire life so he could meet the Lord, and now that he's met Him he would never want to leave Him. He wouldn't come back, Patrick. He is happy. He is fulfilled."

Patrick said that those same words now applied to Alice and me, to our family, and to Danny himself. No matter how hard we begged, Danny wouldn't want to come back either. Now he was truly home.

For to me life is Christ, and death is gain.
(Phillippians: 1-21)

So many people spoke of Danny's transformation after being ordained a priest and his joy in beginning to serve the Church and her people as a priest. By nature Danny was upbeat and happy, a friend to all, full of fun, fully alive, and fully in love with the Lord now his smile was brighter, his gait quicker and his wit a bit sharper Throughout that long and difficult week his joyful spirit infused our home, helping to dispel the gloom. Deo Gratias.

Is not the Lord in the midst of us? No evil
can come upon us! (Micah 3:11)

At one point, Father Michael Drea took me aside in our dining room. He had been an upperclassman when Danny entered the seminary, and he preceded Danny as a Seminarian Intern at St. Mary of the Nativity in Scituate, MA. Father Mike had just one message for me: "Remember, Mr. Kennedy, he is a priest forever!" He repeated the phrase several times, with increasing emphasis, and its full force struck me. Even though I had heard the verse hundreds of time, after listening to Father Drea's emphatic message, it was as if I was hearing it for the first time.

"The Lord has sworn and will not change his mind: "You are a priest forever, in the line of Melchizedek."
(Psalm 110:4)

Seeing our loss from the perspective of eternity was the only way to begin making sense of things. Yes, death could take Danny from us, but it could not undo the sacred tie of Holy Orders, and the man who had loved to foster vocations while here on earth would surely carry on the same ministry when he reached Heaven. As Father Joe Mazzone recalls, "The night after Father Dan died, I told Mr. Kennedy that I always thought Dan's charism — the special focus or gift, if you will of his priesthood — was to bring others to the priesthood. I told him I thought Dan's mission had really just started, not ended."

Alice found comfort through Monsignor William Helmick, who gave her a copy of a letter Saint Aloysius Gonzaga, SJ wrote to his mother as he lay dying. This young priest had not hesitated to scold his own mother on the topic of death, and Alice appreciated his message. It says in part:

If charity, as Saint Paul says, means "to weep with those who weep and rejoice with those who are glad," then, dearest mother, you shall rejoice exceedingly that God in His grace and His love for you is showing me the path to true happiness, and assuring me that I shall never lose Him. Take care above all things, most honored lady, not to insult God's boundless loving kindness; you would certainly do this if you mourned as dead one living face to face with God, one whose prayers can bring you in your troubles more powerful aid than they ever could on earth. And our parting will not be for long; we shall see each other again in heaven; we shall be united with our Savior; there we shall praise him with heart and soul, sings of his mercies for ever, and enjoys eternal happiness.

It was a typical January day in New England; frigid, and it felt even colder to a family numb with grief. Slowly but surely we thawed and were warmed by our dear friends and our Catholic faith.

When the autopsy result arrived, it showed cardiac arrest: a sudden stoppage of the heart. "Baloney," I thought. It was plain as day that Danny's joy-filled heart had not stopped for a moment — it was still alive and kicking among those who knew him best.

Lying in State

Blessed are they who mourn, for they will be comforted. (Matthew 5:4)

Every funeral entails countless decisions, and Danny's was especially complicated. His final earthly race would take his body through two states and in and out of two churches. "It never was easy to slow that boy down," I thought.

People stepped forward with eager offers of help. Danny's good friend Dave Russell, the Director of a Funeral Home in nearby Brockton, handled all the funeral arrangements. Father Brian Manning, Danny's longtime mentor and close friend, Pastor of St. Mary of the Nativity in Scituate, where Danny interned, coordinated arrangements with the Archdiocese Pastoral Center. Father Michael Lawlor, our pastor at St. Joseph in Needham, graciously provided St. Joseph's Church for the wake and funeral. Father Lawlor also established close communication with the Parish Choir, and various ministries to facilitate these events.

At last the final schedule was set. The body would lie in state for public viewing at St. Joseph Church on Thursday, January 31st. The Funeral Mass was scheduled on Friday, February 1st, the feast of St. Brigid — patroness of the parish which would have been Danny's next assignment — with burial on the following day, February 2nd next to my parents at St. Mary's Cemetery in Westfield, Massachusetts.

Alice noticed that February 1st was also the birth date of her late mother, who in her senior years asked, "Danny is going to become a priest, isn't he?" We were mystified at her remark as it came from an unlikely source. Vocations had not been a topic of discussion in our house and to have it brought up by Alice's mother who resided in western Massachusetts was startling. Additionally, our hardheaded, penalty-prone hockey player had multiple adolescent interests and we didn't see a priestly vocation on his list of priorities— but time proved her right.

Deep indeed is the wisdom of the maternal heart.

Boston's Auxiliary Bishop Walter J. Edyvean received Father Daniel J. Kennedy's body into St. Joseph Church at 2:00 p.m. on January 31, 2008.

At 2:00pm friends were already lining up for the visitation which was scheduled to commence at 3:00pm; soon there was a long line of weeping friends extending down Highland Ave, waiting patiently in bitter cold weather to enter St. Joseph's Church to commiserate with our family as well as the many Archdiocesan priests who joined us. Because of the extreme cold, people were invited to sit in the pews while waiting to pay their respects. Soon every pew was filled and still the line extended outside the church and down Highland Avenue.

We were told that many mourners waited in excess of three hours to pay their respects.. Franciscan Friars from St. Anthony's Shrine, Dominicans from Providence College, including Dominican Brother Kevin O'Connell Danny's close friend from his undergraduate days who was now confined to wheel chair, and the entire Catholic Memorial Hockey Team commiserated with our family.

Alice and I greeted hundreds of people that evening. Several years later, a young seminarian came up to me and said happily, "Mr. Kennedy, I took your advice." I had no idea who he was and bluntly asked, "What advice?" He explained that at the wake he introduced himself as a former classmate of Danny's who had since left the seminary. Standing next to the casket, I had emphatically instructed him, "Go back to the seminary!" He did; and four years later Father Eric Cadin was ordained a priest in the Archdiocese of Boston. Deo gratias! In 2015, Father Eric was appointed one of the full-time vocation directors in the Archdiocese of Boston!

On the morning of the wake, Alice woke up with a severe cold/flu and it was doubtful whether she would be able to attend the wake and if so, we wondered if she could endure more than a short stay. When Alice saw the magnitude of the crowd she disregarded her own personal discomfort and was determined to stand with us for the entire service. While I considered that amazing, she was so sick that evening that I was concerned she may not be well enough to attend the Funeral Mass the next day.

The next morning, however, I was shocked and pleasantly surprised to see that Alice was no longer sick. She was in perfect health. She had weathered what was apparently a '24 hour storm' which had not deterred her from standing 'tall' for over eight consecutive hours. Her magnificent maternal strength pulled her through with flying colors. Truly, the Lord does provide protection and grace for mothers.

At the lying-in-state ceremony, Father Dan's great friend Father Matt Westcott offered a few remarks of remembrance. Father Matt was speechless in our home the night of Danny's death, but his profound words at the wake proved he had reached an understanding with God since that dark night. Father Matt reminded us that when we cannot understand, we simply must trust in God's plan:

"Our Lord's love for Dan is infinite. For all of the tragedy of this loss, God will use it to build up His Kingdom and to show forth His Glory. The building up of the Kingdom of God was Dan's mission as a priest in this life. It remains his mission now that he is a priest forever with Our Lord, the Eternal High Priest."

Throughout St. Joseph's Church heads were nodding with affirmative approval as Father Matt spoke:

"Father Dan loved a good time with his family and friends. He loved practical jokes, and giving those he loved a hard time. But most of all he loved being a priest and serving the people of God that, as he told me many times, he had a great love for and wanted to serve."

"Dan died too young. We feel robbed, but if there is any joy to be found in this awful moment it is in the knowledge that Dan died a happy priest, who loved, and was loved by, many people. And there is supreme comfort in the knowledge that he is forever with God, where every tear has been wiped away."

I was enormously proud of our entire family on that seemingly endless day. We all managed to stay on our feet and thank each person who came to pay respect to Dan. The visitation was enervating and emotionally draining, but with each expression of respect and love we felt invigorated and empowered.

In order to accommodate the throngs of grieving people the wake was extended. Shortly after 10:00 p.m. the line dissipated and we slowly proceeded to our cars. Once all family members were safely secured in their cars, I slipped back into church for one last look. Standing in the back of the now darkened church, a lone light beamed down on the altar, its rays illuminating Danny's earthly body, lying at rest at the foot of the Altar.

My mind flashed back to the day he was born, when he lay so peacefully in his hospital basinet, blanketed in white and blue while a statue of Mary stood nearby. Now, thirty-four years later, I gazed at a grown man, a priest of Christ, lying peacefully; robed in the red chasuble he had worn to celebrate his First Mass of Thanksgiving at this Altar just eight months ago. Nearby, the statue of Mary seemed to be standing guard. Our boy was in good hands; time for me to go home.

Requiem

Mourn with those who mourn. (Sirach 7:34b)

On Friday, February 1, 2008, the Feast Day of St. Brigid, the Patroness of the Parish in South Boston where he had been scheduled to begin his tenure as Parochial Vicar on February 5, 2008, a crowd of grieving people filled St. Joseph's Church in Needham to celebrate Father Dan's entry into Eternal Life.

In Winthrop at St. John the Evangelist parish, where Father Dan had been assigned as Parochial Vicar for eight months — and where he had just bid the parish farewell — a bus was chartered to carry parishioners to the Funeral Mass. Others would travel by car to Needham to say their 'second' goodbye within a week.

St. Joseph's Choir led the congregation in singing the Navy Hymn as we followed Lieutenant Daniel J Kennedy's coffin into the church. Interestingly, the hymns he had selected to be sung at his First Mass of Thanksgiving were suitable for his Funeral Mass. Strange! Among the Hymn's that were sung; 'You Are Mine'; by David Haas, was one his favorite liturgical hymns. It is especially fitting that it was sung at both of these important 'liturgical services'.

St. Joseph's Church was over flowing with bereaved people amongst who were a cardinal, four bishops and over 200 priests. The principal celebrant was Cardinal Seán Patrick O'Malley, OFM cap., Archbishop of Boston, who, on May 26, 2007, ordained Father Daniel J Kennedy and Father Matthew J Westcott. Father Westcott, proclaimed the Gospel, and Bishop Robert F Hennessey offered the Homily.

Bishop Hennessey, as a parochial vicar at St. Joseph Parish when Danny was an altar boy, had introduced Danny to Eucharistic Adoration. Setting a somber tone, Bishop Hennessey said, "We do not come here today to celebrate a life. There will be time for that. We come here today to mourn a death." His words of remembrance shone with his love for a joyful man and boy who was proud to be gifted with a vocation to the priesthood of Christ.

At the end of the Funeral Mass, I rose to offer a few words of remembrance even though my family strenuously objected to the idea. Jack begged me allow him to offer a eulogy on behalf of the family, which was vociferously seconded by Alice, who knew my tendency to weep at funerals. Father Lawlor, our pastor, attempted to prevail upon me to recant my plan, as he, tactfully, pointed out Cardinal O'Malley would need adequate time to render his own remarks. Danny was not the only stubborn redhead in our house. I had a clear sense of what needed to be presented and was determined to fulfill my parental responsibility — trusting the Holy Spirit to guide my tongue and keep tears away.

I was convinced that a plea for vocations was the best way to honor Father Dan, who spent years running from his vocation before finally acquiescing and embracing it with pride and joy. Ever since Father Dan died people had been asking me, "What can we do for you?" My answer to them was exactly what I now told that packed church:

"For your consideration I would suggest: every morning when you get out of bed, offer your entire day for an increase in vocations to the priesthood. Please constantly pray for vocations to the priesthood. Thank you."

What more needed saying? Everyone present knew that Father Dan had been fully alive, fully human, fully in love with the Lord, and brilliant at permeating the aroma of Christ (2 Corinthians 2:15). Father Dan knew well that everyone, whether they realize it or not, craves Christ. He was determined to open those hearts and those minds to the truth of Christ's love for them. I told a few stories of Dan's inimitable blend of deep faith and high humor, then ended with the lesson Job learned only through suffering: *"The Lord giveth, and the Lord taketh away; blessed be the name of the Lord!" (Job 1:21)*

At that point I returned to my place in the pew next to Alice. Shortly afterward Cardinal O'Malley rose to approach the lectern.

He appeared deeply moved. He began by recalling the last time he saw Dan, when he had asked, "How are you doing Dan?" and he received the happy reply, "I love being a priest." The Cardinal faltered and in a choked voice said, "Sometimes the best homily is a short homily." Abruptly he returned to the presider's chair.

Precious in the eyes of the Lord is the death of his faithful.
(Psalm 116)

If there were a 'dry eye' in the church it was no longer 'dry' as the entire presbyterate in attendance ascended the Sanctuary steps and sang the customary Hymn sung at Funeral Masses for priests; 'Salve Regina'.

Salve Regina, Mater Misericordiae
Vita dulcedo et spes nostra salve
Ad te clamamus, exsules filii Hevae
Ad te suspiramus, gementes et flentes
In hac lacrimarum valle, Eia, ergo, advocata nostra
illos tuos misericordes oculos ad nos converte

Et Iesum, benedictum fructum ventris tui
Nobis post hoc exsilium ostende
O clemens, O pia, O dulcis, Virgo Maria

Final Commitment

He will wipe every tear from their eyes. (Revelation 21:4a)

On February 2, 2008, Father Daniel J. Kennedy was interred next to his paternal grandparents, Patrick Joseph and Eileen Margaret Kennedy, in St. Mary's Cemetery in Westfield, Massachusetts. Russell-Pica Funeral Home of Brockton arranged with the Massachusetts State Police to escort the funeral procession on the 90-mile trek along the Massachusetts Turnpike. Many of our 'western Mass' friends joined the 'eastern Mass' contingent for the Committal Services.

In the snowy cemetery, Danny's longtime friend Bishop Emeritus Joseph F. Maguire of the Springfield Diocese, read the Committal Prayers, assisted by Springfield's then current Bishop Timothy A. McDonnell and Danny's diaconate mentor, Father Brian F. Manning. As the elderly Bishop Maguire — formerly a noted athlete at Boston College — painstakingly navigated the snow-packed ground to reach the graveside and bless the casket, we could see plainly his love for this young athlete, who has run his final race.

Following the interment our family hosted a luncheon at the nearby Storrowton Tavern, in West Springfield in the same ballroom where we held our Wedding Reception, almost 40 years ago, to the day, in 1968. So many memories!

Dozens of Danny's friends traveled great distances to say goodbye to the man who never lacked for a big smile, caring eyes, frequently accompanied with a gregarious pat on the back and always with a firm handshake. In that vein, Jack set a happy tone as Master of Ceremonies. Several of his friends regaled us with tales of Danny's escapades and his gift for finding humor just about everywhere. Their joy-filled recollections were a precious gift for which Alice and I remain grateful.

A parishioner from St. Mary of the Nativity wrote recently, "My children loved him dearly, as did the entire Catholic community in Scituate. To this day I miss his laugh — it is high on my list of what I want to see and hear when I join him in heaven."

We share her feelings. Like Alice and me, Danny's siblings — Katie, Patti, Anne Marie, and Jack — we believe that Danny died in God's grace and has been welcomed by his friend, Jesus Christ. As believers, we can "rejoice and be glad" that he has reached Eternal Life, but as mere human beings; we miss him.

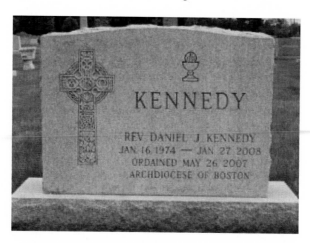

Chapter 2: "It's a Boy?"

For a child is born to us, a son is given to us. (Isaiah 9:5a)

All five times when I brought Alice to Providence Hospital in Holyoke to deliver a baby I paced miles between the waiting room and the chapel, unable to settle in either place. In 1969 I walked for Katie, in 1970 for Patti, in 1972 for Anne Marie, in 1974 for Danny and in 1975 for Jackie. Each time my pacing ended in tears: tears of joy at receiving a new baby but mostly tears of thanks that my beloved Alice's nine-month odyssey had ended safely.

After living in a household of females for a few years, I was accustomed to being presented by the nurses with a baby girl. I was mildly surprised, not overly elated, when our nurse showed me tightly wrapped baby in a blue blanket on January 16, 1974. Before I could truly enjoy our new son, my paramount thought was, as always, Alice.

When I was allowed to visit Alice in the recovery room, per usual, I was crying. Immediately she gave me what had almost become, an annual response; "Why are you crying? Is the baby all right?" I assured her the baby was fine but the issue is; "How are you?" She assured me she was fine and was pleased to have a baby boy.

I told her that I had already seen 'Kevin Michael'. Prior to every trip to Providence Hospital we had two names selected – one if the baby was a girl and one if the baby was a boy. The boy's name that had been selected since 1969 was Kevin Michael.

Alice looked at me and unequivocally said; "He will be named after his father; his name is Daniel Joseph". I must admit, any opposition from me to Alice's affirmative remark was weak if not, non-existent. Years later in respect to his paternal grandfather Danny would select 'Patrick' as his Confirmation name and he was always pleased to identify himself as; Daniel Joseph Patrick Kennedy.

Everyone has experienced proud fathers trying to vicariously relive athletic feats through their sons, and to some extent I plead guilty to that allegation, but my hope was different in one respect. As I boy I had always yearned to be on the Altar and to serve Mass. Our family's parish, Our Lady of Hope Parish in Springfield, MA, mandated that Altar Servers must attend the parish school.

I never forgot a poem that my father regularly recited to me when I was a little boy; 'What I couldn't be, *little boy*, I want *you* to be, *little boy*," etc. I thought to myself, wouldn't it be grand, if at some point, Alice and I were blessed with a son who might someday serve Mass? (Prior to Vatican II girls were not authorized to serve Mass).

Granted, it would be years before this newborn baby boy would be old enough to don a server's cassock, assuming of course that he would be interested in serving Mass. Did it ever cross my mind this little baby might one day become a priest? Not for a second. Religious vocations simply had never been in our family genealogy.

When I came home to share the news with our daughters I was taken aback with their reaction. After awakening from sleep to learn of baby Danny's arrival, our three-year-old daughter Patti, with disdain dripping from her mouth, incredulously shouted, "It's a boy? It's a *boy*?" Katie, disappointedly, flopped back onto her pillow, scoffing and mumbling "A brother?" Girls were familiar to our daughters so they considered this an 'all-girl family'. Anne Marie was only two years old and still too young to enunciate a dissenting opinion to arrival of our newest family member.

Eventually, acceptance was achieved when another brother, John Francis, was born a year and a half later. Danny broke the streak of girls so Jackie was enthusiastically welcomed by his three sisters. In a large family, the caboose generally occupies a premier place in the parental heart and Jackie was no exception. Even though Jackie was not a redhead he was the 'fair-haired boy'. Alice and I were blessed with three daughters close in age and two sons close in age; intra family companionship would never be in want.

Our daughters were outgoing and competitive. Their proclivity to tease as well as their accomplished athletic skills impacted their younger brothers. Jackie was somewhat insulated from their tantalizing antics but not Danny. When Danny was four or five years old one of his sisters told him she overheard Mom and Dad discussing a plan to abandon him at a local amusement park. Immediately, Danny, frightened to the core, confronted the alleged perpetrator of the plan, his mother.

Alice, not one to procrastinate, quickly convened the girls, corroborated the concocted story, and emphatically laid the law down to them. To my knowledge there were never any future fabricated threats; threats, yes, fabrication, no.

Between their banter and bamboozling, Danny turned out equally feisty and quick-witted. He became a redheaded charmer who could give as well as he received and, in turn, he showed little Jackie how to push back. Jack was somewhat insulated from the female animosity as he was not the culprit that broke the streak of girls. Did their in-house teasing turn into scuffles? Absolutely.

Charting the Course

As for me and my household, we will serve the Lord. (Joshua 24:15)

Five children in six years; difficult as it may have been at times Alice was definitely up to that task. She never stopped moving, a human dynamo; truly, she was poetry in motion; implementing systems and doling out non-negotiable responsibilities. She ran our family like Maria ran the von Trapp Family in The Sound of Music; regimentation strategically augmented with love. No, Alice was not a former nun but she certainly utilized the innate discipline she acquired from the Sisters of St Joseph. All five kids, and me as well, were assigned specific tasks and woe to us if we fell short of her expectations! As one of Katie's friends, Dr. Diane Dermarderosian, said recently; "Mrs. Kennedy was a no nonsense person".

At one point when a baby sitter we engaged so we could enjoy a brief respite of peace and quiet was asked how she liked babysitting for the Kennedy Kids she replied; "It's not babysitting, it's more like taming lions." Do you think Alice's high-powered energy was inherited by the infamous five?

Alice and I never stopped thanking God for blessing us with five wonderful kids. Every night when I knelt down to say my evening prayers God always heard the same plea from me; "Thank you, Lord, for the gift of Katie, Patti, Anne Marie, Danny, and Jackie. Please, Lord, give Alice and me the Grace to bring up *Your* children the way *You* want us to bring up *Your* children." My intent was to continually recognize God's gift of custodial care and to pray for His constant support.

Neither Alice nor I badgered our children with an onslaught of religiosity. Our strategy was to lead by example. Both of us were active in parish activities. Alice organized children liturgies and volunteered at St. Mary's School in Westfield and St. Joseph's School in Needham. She also served each school as a 'Room Mother.' Later in life, Alice was appointed to co-chair a Catholic Conference to enhance elementary education in the Archdiocese of Boston along with Auxiliary Bishop Daniel A. Hart.

I was not as actively involved as Alice but I did serve on the Lector Team and on the Parish Council at St. Mary's in Westfield and St. Joseph's in Needham. The Friars at St. Anthony's Shrine on 'Arch Street' in Downtown Boston also had to endure my presence as a Noontime Lector and Extraordinary Minister.

Advent prepared our family for Christmas Eve arrival of the Babe of Bethlehem and the Lenten Season prepared us for the Resurrection of Our Lord Jesus Christ. These canonical seasons enabled us to continually integrate Catholicism into the daily life of our young family. It is only in retrospection that we perceive the unique and important impact of these most holy times upon all our children. From adolescent to teenager to young adult, Catholicism became an anchor for all of our five spirited kids.

Danny, like his siblings, grew emotionally and spiritually year by year, and it is only in reflecting back that I realize we may have been too engrossed with day to day life to visualize Danny in the same light as others perceived him. Every so often someone would remark about his spiritual awareness or by asking, "Do you think Danny might have a vocation?" Of course we were pleased by the observation but neither Alice nor I focused on the future for any of our kids as we were focused on doing 'today's work today'. *Do not worry about tomorrow, tomorrow will take care of itself.* (Matthew 6:34)

All we saw was a cheerful redhead bubbling, happy, enthusiastic and, like his mother, with nonstop energy!

Out of Necessity; Physical Exercise (aka Sports and More Sports)

I was my father's child, tender, the darling of my mother... (Psalm 4:3)

One after another, almost annually, each child was enrolled at St. Mary's Grammar School, our parish school in Westfield, Massachusetts. Danny eagerly followed in his big sisters' footsteps, becoming a good student and joining as many activities as we would agree to, especially sports and service projects.

The winter of 1978 will long be remembered as a winter of record snowfall. With so much snow I was concerned the entire family would be afflicted with claustrophobia. Eventually I had a brainstorm; I could freeze the back yard and would have an outlet for the kids: our own skating rink! My idea was an instant hit, giving the kids an outlet for their energy and providing Alice a break from their being cooped up indoors. Soon the girls were skating well enough to start figure skating classes and, although only six, Danny became a strong skater as well. For his 6th birthday I purchased hockey skates, sticks and a brilliant red helmet for his 6th birthday. It turned out to be a sport would play for the rest of his life.

Soon I registered Danny on the under 8 Westfield Mites Cam-four Indians, entry into the Western Mass Youth Hockey League. As a six year old, two years younger than most of his teammates, Danny was at a decided disadvantage which ultimately inured to his benefit. Through observation and hard work his hockey skills improved immeasurably. At the end of the season it was obvious that he benefited playing with older teammates.

The coach of the Westfield Mites, Clarence "Moose" Mathews, was pleased to have a beginner who listened attentively and worked hard, and Danny was soon aiding in the team's wins. After that first season, Coach Mathews offered me his considered opinion: "Danny could develop into a top flight hockey player," as his ability indicated the potential to play hockey at a high level. "But," Coach Mathews continued, "I think it's more likely he'll become a priest."

I was floored. A man who was not even Catholic considered Danny a prospective priest? What had we been missing? What on earth had Danny said or done to prompt that observation? Coach Mathews said it was the way he interacted with his teammates and concern he had for other players who may have felt badly if they played poorly. In retrospect it may have been that Danny blessed himself before going on the ice. He may have noted from watching baseball games on TV that some batters bless themselves as they enter the batter's box. I truly don't know.

Many years later I recalled that, as a young boy in Westfield, Danny formed the habit of making the Sign of the Cross on his forehead. From the time he played Youth Hockey in Westfield, no matter how far he advanced in the sport, he never took a shift on the ice without, *purportedly, adjusting his helmet* — he was surreptitiously tracing the cross on his forehead. As an adult, after pulling up in front of our house in his car or for that matter anywhere, he would remain in the car for a few seconds pretending to adjust the rearview mirror, but quickly making the Sign of the Cross on his forehead. If he received a telephone call, prior to picking up the receiver he would brush back his hair, covertly crossing his forehead. It was as if Danny felt a need to engage his friend Jesus in every aspect of his life and to call on Him for protection. In view of his propensity of making the Sign of the Cross especially when coming to visit us, I would suspect, as he pulled his car into Jack and Beth's driveway in Simsbury, CT, that he made the Sign of the Cross on his forehead. *"This shall be your armor...the sign of the cross on your forehead..."* (St. John Chrysostom; Instructions to Catechumens)

In the spring both Danny and Jackie were invited to play in the Town of Agawam Tee Ball League. This was their introduction into a baseball environment. The boys loved to swing the bat, whack the baseball and run, run, and run. In was another win-win as they enjoyed it and it helped them expend energy. When they arrived home, they slept, soundly!

In November of 1980, our entire family attended the priestly ordination of Deacon Francis E. Reilly as a priest for the Diocese of Springfield. The children knew Fran well, because the Reilly family lived next door to my parents and, as a seminarian, Fran made it a point to stop at Gram and Pop's house for a visit on Christmas Day.

After the Ordination concluded, the consecrator, Bishop Joseph F. Maguire, stopped to shake hands with us and, peering down at our wiggly six- and four-year-old boys, he asked, "Do you think one of these boys might become a priest someday, Dan?"

I politely responded, "I hope so, Bishop." My reply precipitated another momentary glance from Bishop Maguire as he digested my cooperatively phased response.

To our delight, Father Fran's first assignment was the Church of St. Mary in Westfield. Consequently, Father Reilly was a frequent visitor to our home. Father Fran was a fine athlete so he enjoyed bringing his hockey skates for a game with the kids on the backyard rink. Danny not only looked forward have Father Reilly skate with the Kennedy Kids he also looked to the children's Masses at St. Mary's. He was thrilled that Father Fran invited all the children to enter the sanctuary and stand around the Altar as he celebrated Mass. Danny was quick to rush up and find a good spot close to his friend, the skating priest.

Nearly thirty years later a member of the St. John the Evangelist Youth Group in Winthrop remembered Father Dan's version. Alyssa Trinidad wrote: "He would always call the children to come up to the Altar during family masses and give a great Homily to those youngsters. I always found it funny when he would wait until the Sanctuary was almost full, and then he would say, 'There are still some good seats left.'"

What Coach Mathews had seen in Danny mystified me until a year later, when I had a preview of my son's spiritual life. It occurred on the night Danny scored six goals in the Westfield Mites decisive win over the South Hadley Mites at the Fitzpatrick Rink in Holyoke. I was thrilled that his skating ability enabled him to completely dominate the offensive zone and I looked forward to recap his exploits on our drive home after the game. Contrary to my expectation, there was little or no mention of the game. Danny was content to silently gaze at the stars in the sky. He continued to marvel at the brightness of the stars as we descended East Mountain Road in

Westfield when he suddenly spoke and said, "I wonder what God is doing tonight?"

I was absolutely stunned at his remark. At the summit of his young athletic career his thoughts were clearly on higher things than regaling about his hockey exploits. When I composed my thoughts I merely said, "God is probably pleased that you scored six goals".

Could his observation be construed as a prayer? Could the view of stars from a mountain road prompt a prayer? I do not know.

Present yourself to me on top of the mountain....
(Exodus 34:1-3)

Another clue that contemplation was prevalent was in evidence in his self-imposed prayer time after Mass. Whereas I always wanted to rush out of church after Sunday Mass and load the kids into the car, Danny retained the St Mary's Parish tradition of kneeling in private prayer at the conclusion of Mass. He continued to maintain that tradition after we relocated to Needham; the rest of us did not. I was fully aware that he treasured a private prayer life so I knew better than to intrude into his privacy and he never volunteered information about those private prayers. At times, for me, it was exasperating as we were generally on a tight schedule and we did not have time to spare. In his mind, our concern for expediency was irrelevant.

Both Alice and I, cradle Catholics, were faithful in worship and active in parish activities. Alice was deeply involved in several aspects of St. Mary's School and, subsequently, St. Joseph School. I was a Parish Lector and a member of the Parish Council at St. Mary's and St. Joseph's. We prayed daily, went to Mass and Confession regularly, and our children attended parochial schools. We tried to live our faith in an unassuming manner and felt no need to preach about it. Priests often came to our home for dinner, but that was just friendship, not some covert attempt to sell our children on the religious life.

As our kids grew up they witnessed firsthand that priests are just like everybody else: they like to laugh, sing, skate, play golf, tell jokes — and eat. When Father Tony Creane, Pastor of St. Mary's, came for dinner or whether he just 'popped in' after a tough day, he would bring his golf clubs and the two of us would chip a few balls in the backyard. If Father David Joyce, Parochial Vicar at St. Mary's, was our guest we would gather around the piano to hear him sing Irish songs. When Father Reilly graced our abode he would bring either his hockey skates or his guitar; it was always a festive occasion.

There were occasions when, for business reasons, Alice was invited to accompany me to various conventions so we engaged the Sisters of St. Joseph to 'baby-sit' our kids. We also maintained this strategy when we moved to Needham; the Sisters of Charity from Halifax, Nova Scotia, were our 'security blankets'.

Our entire family loved Westfield. The school, sports and neighbors were extraordinary. We developed a lifelong relationship with our next door neighbors Richard and Janice Butcher and their four children. Occasionally, a Dominican Missionary who was serving in Kenya, would visit our next-door neighbor the Butcher Family. During the week, while I was at the office, Father Joseph Desmond, OP, would offer Mass and Mrs. Butcher invited Alice and the five kids to attend the Mass. Even though the Butchers had four children for some reason, at the conclusion of the Mass, Father Desmond always offered Danny the opportunity to 'blow out the candles'. Danny was thrilled and he always looked forward to Father Desmond's visits next door so he could do his job; 'blow out the candles."

Although it was never discussed, Alice and I often wondered why Father Desmond selected Danny to blow out the candles and not one of the Butcher boys. (Perhaps Danny was second, or third, or fourth choice)

Many years later, as a student at Providence College, Danny, a member of a college service club, visited a Nursing Home in Providence, Rhode Island. Danny noticed a door tag: Father Joseph Desmond, OP. It was the friend of the Butcher family! Danny immediately knocked on the door, entered the room, and introduced himself as the former candle-blower-outer from Westfield. Their friendship was rekindled on the spot. A few weeks later, Father Desmond passed away and Dan requested approval to serve the Funeral Mass at St. Thomas Aquinas Chapel at the Dominican Priory — at the conclusion of the Mass, Dan blew out the candles!

Summer in Westfield meant our kids spent hours at the Cross Street Playground, where one of the summer supervisors was Mike Kelley, an offensive lineman for the University of Notre Dame football team. Danny played baseball under Mike's tutelage, and in the fall he looked for him on television when a Notre Dame game was televised. After his friendship with Mike commenced Danny announced that he was going to study hard so he too could attend the University of Notre Dame. Alice and I were pleased that at such a young age he established a clear goal for himself. With his brain, energy, and athleticism along with his stubborn streak, Danny seemed to be pointing himself in the right direction.

Uprooted

If the root is holy, so are the branches. (Romans 11:16b)

In September 1981, my employer, General Accident Insurance Company offered me the opportunity to assume responsibility for the operation of the Boston Branch office. Although the benefits and the challenge were enticing I had reservations about relocating the entire family. I felt that accepting this opportunity would be at the expense of inconveniencing six others.

In addition, the company stipulated that, if I accepted the position I should plan on assuming the responsibilities within two weeks! Alice assured me that she could handle the day-to-day family duties as well as facilitating the logistics of the relocation. Most emphatically, she assured me that the move would ultimately broaden the kids and that, it would inure to their benefit. Reticence resolved.

Alice bore the brunt of the transition to Eastern Massachusetts so, as not to over burden her, I decided to commute daily to the North Shore of Boston. That plan worked well. I would leave Westfield at 5am and I was back home at 7pm to listen to 'school stories' and to assist Alice in putting the kids to bed.

While I was in the office Alice took immediate action in locating a community for us in the Boston area. In addition to house hunting she negotiated with the transfer company, Merrill Lynch in selling our Westfield home as well as effectively handling a multitude of other aspects of the relocation. Somehow she was able to sort and pack all our worldly goods, while at the same time; she balanced homework assignments and sports schedules. Within a few weeks

Alice found a home in Needham that she absolutely loved so we were full steam ahead with our transition.

We were fortunate in that our new parish in Needham, St. Joseph's, had a parish school. When Alice stopped in to register our kids she was informed two of the grades we would need for the kids were filled. Upon being told that two children would have to attend the public school, Alice replied succinctly: "All or none." And lo, it came to pass that all five Kennedys were enrolled at St. Joseph School under the tutelage of the Sisters of Charity from Halifax.

Our three daughters made their First Holy Communion at St. Mary's and beginning with Danny on May 1, 1982, at age eight, both boys made their First Holy Communion at St Joseph's. Because Danny exhibited far more excitement and enthusiasm in preparing for his First Holy Communion than any of his sisters before him, Alice and I decided to reward his intense anticipation. We told him he could choose his own blazer, and he selected a green blazer (probably the only young boy on record to wear a green blazer at his First Holy Communion) *Go Irish!*

My long-cherished dream came true when Danny asked us to register him for training as Altar Server training at St. Josephs. Almost immediately he began to love serving Mass and he would serve as often as possible. He even volunteered to serve at the 8:30 Saturday morning Mass. His enthusiasm and dedication impressed the pastor, Father Francis Connors, and the other parish priests. Danny recalled later that Father Connors asked him if he thought he might "join them in the priesthood" someday. Danny also mentioned "a couple of the nuns I had in elementary school asked me and my classmates regularly if we had ever considered priesthood." When he grew into adulthood, Danny too advocated 'asking' young men to consider a vocation to the priesthood. It is Marketing 101, he argued: If seeds are not planted, how will they grow and bear fruit?

Ask and it will be given to you…. (Matthew 7:7).

One evening at dinner, I mentioned I planned to attend the St. Joseph Parish Retreat. Danny (only) asked if he could come along so he accompanied me. The visiting priest, Father Paul Trammontozzi, ofm singled Danny out for coming and said, "I am impressed with that little boy who has nightly attended this retreat with his father," the priest commented in his homily. "He seems so attentive. I hope I live long enough to be in attendance at his ordination." Another seed had been planted. Although at long last I was starting to see a pattern. Perhaps I was wrong but my thought was 'don't pile on - let God's plan play out'.

Throughout his grade school years Danny balanced academic requirements, extracurricular activities, serving Mass and playing sports. Practices and games for the Needham Mites in the Greater Boston Youth Hockey League, Needham Little League, and the St. Joseph Basketball program were particularly time consuming. At the conclusion of the his first season on the Needham Mites, Frances Fleming, wife of the team's coach, Kevin Fleming, told me that she thought Danny would ultimately become a priest. I thought her remark quite interesting if not perplexing, in that his hockey coach in Westfield made the same observation.

The various sports programs also expected that the young players would participate in annual fundraising projects. One year Danny's labors in hawking raffle tickets enabled him to win 'Salesman of the Season' recognition; he won a Thanksgiving turkey. But before Alice could even ask its weight, the turkey flew the coop:

without consulting anyone, Danny donated it to the parish so it could be given to a needy family. Alice was proud of his unprompted generosity. "But," she lamented, "I certainly could have used that bird."

Old Friends, Best Friends

Faithful friends are a sturdy shelter; whoever finds one finds a treasure.
(Sirach 6:14)

From an early age Danny gravitated toward seniors. He was comfortable with the elderly and showed a natural empathy, especially when visiting housebound persons. When we visited our Kennedy relatives in Springfield he appeared to be captivated with his great-aunt Betty Kennedy, who was incapacitated by Parkinson's disease. In Westfield, he frequently visited Mrs. Clemons whose home was on the opposite side of Falley Drive and who was house bound. In Needham, Danny regularly visited another neighbor, Mrs. Kelly, an elderly widow living alone, directly across the street from us on Woodlawn Ave.

As she counted heads before dinner or before a trip to one of many different daily destinations Alice would often call out, "Where's Danny?" Not in the yard with Jack and the dog; not in the driveway where Anne Marie was perfecting her three-pointer at the basketball hoop; not in the family room coloring with Patti or reading with Katie. Where was Danny? "Oh, he's probably visiting Mrs. Kelly," someone would guess. It was a safe bet. "Religion that is pure…is this: to care for orphans and widows…" (James 1:27)

Danny never just popped in and out of his elderly friends' homes: he liked to sit and converse at length. We never knew what was discussed, but often he returned with a pocketful of candy, and his "old friends" also helped out whenever he was peddling raffle tickets.

During the summer months in Dennisport on Cape Cod, he regularly walked around the block to visit with Mrs. Griffin, another elderly housebound, as a redundant Irish relative of mine used to say, "widow woman". A few years later, Mrs. Griffin's daughter, Mary Waldron, called Alice and told her that her mother, then a resident of a nursing home, was thrilled to see Danny serving Mass on Boston Catholic Television. The Director of BCTV knew how much he loved to serve Mass so he invited him to serve Mass on TV and, of course, he was thrilled. His red hair must have contributed to a momentary restoration of Mrs. Griffin's cognitive skills.

Mrs. Clayton Lester lived around the corner from us in Needham and she became another member of Danny's "old friends club" A regular at the Saturday morning Mass at St. Joseph's, Mrs. Lester always sat in the first pew and she gave Danny a sweet smile whenever he came out to serve Mass. It wasn't long before Danny started sneaking a little wave back to Mrs. Lester. Over time they became close friends, and Mrs. Lester prayed that this cheerful Altar Server would someday become a priest of God.

Twenty years later, well into her nineties, and a resident of an assisted living home, Mrs. Lester returned to her customary front row seat at the Church of St. Joseph's. Her daughter read in the parish bulletin that her little redheaded friend from years past was going to celebrate his First Mass of Thanksgiving and she insisted on being in attendance. Mrs. Lester arrived at St. Joseph's Church 45 minutes before Mass to make certain she could confiscate her customary front row seat. Father Dan was in the Sacristy preparing for the Mass when he was informed that Mrs. Lester was present for the occasion; excitedly, he rushed out to greet her. Mrs. Lester told him that attending his First Mass was the answer to years of prayers.

A few weeks after his First Mass I received a phone call from a local author requesting Danny's telephone number. He informed me that he heard about a senior citizen who had prayed for Danny's vocation and was surprisingly in attendance at his First Mass. He informed me that he wanted to publish an article about such a unique occurrence. When I told Danny about the call he vehemently refused to be interviewed for the article. Even though he portrayed gregariousness he was a private person at heart.

One of the parishioners at St. Joseph's who recognized something unique about young Danny was Mary MacGillicuddy. Mrs. MacGillicuddy was in charge of St. Joseph's Annual May Crowning of the Blessed Mother and she nominated Danny to crown the Statue of the Blessed Mother. The ensuing furor of the committee was reminiscent to his sister's reaction when he was born, 'no boys need apply'. Never before had a boy been selected for this honor. In spite of the opposition his advocate prevailed, adamant that

Danny exhibited a unique reverence for the sacraments and, for the Blessed Mother, thus he fully deserved the honor.

Two decades later, after his ordination, Father Dan wrote gratefully to Mary MacGillicuddy (and her husband, Tom) "Your prayers and support since I was a little boy, especially your efforts in recommending me to crown the statue of the Blessed Mother, have been instrumental in making priesthood a reality for me, a most unworthy servant." Danny never forgot an act of friendship, and he never missed a chance to say thanks.

Both at home and away, our young son seemed to know innately not just how to be a good student and team player, but how to be a Christian and a friend. Yet another of Danny's "old friends" was my mother. Gram prefaced her high regard for Danny by reiterating that she loved all her grandchildren equally; but, as she told me more than once; "there is just something special about Danny".

Danny's first experience with the death of someone he knew came at age eleven, when my father died. By then he had served many funeral Masses, so had ample opportunity to contemplate the passage from life to eternity; still, the death of someone we have known and loved can test our faith at any age. Pop died two days before Christmas in 1985. Among all the grandchildren Alice thought Danny seemed especially moved — not distraught, but deeply thoughtful. As for me, in the bustle and sorrow of my father's death and burial, I failed to notice Danny's preoccupation. Perhaps this happens with any child who develops spiritual depths: the parents notice mostly in hindsight.

Calls and Silence

I have called you by name: you are mine. (Isaiah 43:1b)

Danny definitely enjoyed sports, but he also was a dedicated student and but he really loved to write. At about age ten he deftly combined two of them in an essay about Bobby Orr, the former Boston Bruins Hockey Team Hall of Fame defenseman. "When I am older I want to be a priest and a professional hockey player like Bobby Orr," he wrote. "Then I can play hockey and say Bobby Orr's

Funeral Mass." Alice and I thought this was hilarious; we certainly never took it as an opening to discuss vocations. Vocations were still nowhere on our radar.

Every Friday, during Lent, Alice always brought the kids with her to the Stations of the Cross, at St. Joe's. As with any outing involving five children, this Lenten practice increasingly became a struggle. The little boys were restless; the older girls were resentful at having to give up some of their free time after school. As was our family modus operandi, Alice wanted to convey, subliminally, that which is important to parents might someday become important to the kids.

Many parents wonder, "How do we keep our kids Catholic?" No single answer exists. Sending children to Catholic schools may give them a sound understanding of our faith, but faith is a gift from God, not from parents or teachers, a gift they will accept or reject — or perhaps set aside for a time, only to rediscover it later with joy and gratitude for God's Mercy.

Alice and I agreed that we would never force our children to attend church although we certainly hoped and prayed that they would always be faithful. Our plan was to exemplify love for the Catholic faith on a daily basis with the hope that by absorption, a strong faith would be inculcated in each of them.

Our soft-sell approach did seem to positively impact Danny. Occasionally, priests, nuns, and laity would mention that they perceived a possible vocation in him. Those observations were not as visible to us as we lived our daily family life.

The sole exception seemed to be his maternal grandmother, Alice Helen Haggerty, (Nana) who was a convert to Catholicism. When Danny was about fifteen and she was in her eighties, Nana lived with us for a short time. She was ill, frail, and not always clear of mind. One day in a moment of lucidity, she suddenly blurted, "Danny is going to become a priest, isn't he?" Alice and I were astonished. The word vocation was not in our daily vocabulary of possible career paths. One of us replied diplomatically, "We have no idea," changed the subject, and no more was said.

Later we came to sense that Danny might have a calling, but as he was extremely private, we resolved not to mention the topic to him lest he rebel at our unsolicited advice. Did our reluctance to broach the topic of vocation complicate his struggle for discernment? Alice and I hoped he would understand that our silence was not indifference but rather respect for his free will and his judgment. We were convinced that this was a decision he had to reach on his own in prayer, and any intervention from us would be like excited hockey parents offering athletic advice from the stands; counter productive, not at all helpful.

As Danny discovered the hard way, it takes intensive listening before God's call breaks through the noise of this world, so every reminder to young men to listen up, listen hard, listen well is like a good coach pointing them in the right direction. I thank God that Danny found lots of cultivators along the way.

As he told his sister Katie when he announced to her that he was entering St. John's Seminary; "You can't keep God on 'call-waiting' too long". Eventually, he acquiesced.

On the other hand, some years later Father Dan scolded me about keeping silent when I saw a young man devoutly praying at Eucharistic Adoration. "Did you ask if he had considered looking into the seminary?" he asked. "No," I replied, thinking: "Of course not; he was a perfect stranger." Danny shot me that indefatigable glare of his and said; "What is wrong with you?" he demanded.

"Don't you realize it's your obligation to suggest that prayerful young men consider the seminary?"

Quickly I realized that he was right when it comes to encouraging vocations: Don't be shy. Nurture the seed God may have planted with gentleness and dexterity. It is first and foremost God's plan but He does expect us to cultivate the seed.

Day to day family living in the Kennedy household was exciting; it was not as they say, 'a bowl full of jelly' or 'all peaches and cream'. There were some trying times especially with the competitive nature of Danny and Jackie. One Mother's day, Danny and Jackie had a fistfight on our front lawn; Alice was visibly disturbed. Before I could reach them she had grasped both of them by their necks and shipped them off to separate rooms. Another trying incident occurred when they were teenagers, the day Danny received his driver's license. Big brother offered to chauffer Jackie on a short ride around town. When they returned from an abbreviated 'first ride' the two of them were punching each other in the front seat of the car! Alice told them to cease and desist but they ignored her plea for peace.

Alice was no shrinking violet, she believed in fighting fire with fire so with fire in her eyes Alice, literally, swung into action. With her ever-ready toolbox close at hand she grabbed her hammer and proceeded to smash the windshield of the car. Glass splinters flew all over both boys as they cowered in the front seat. Armistice achieved! Both boys were trembling as they sheepishly exited the car as Alice meted out appropriate punishment; confiscation of Danny's Driver's license and prohibition of Jackie's impending Driver Training Lessons.

As a young girl, our next-door neighbor in Westfield, Beth Butcher, said she always loved to go the Kennedy boys' hockey games because during the game, inevitably, a fight would break out. Not a fight amongst the opposing players but a fight between Danny and Jackie! Growing up as the only boy in our family, I could never grasp the ramifications of this form of brotherly love.

Chapter 3: Knights of the Round Table

Train the young in the way they should go; even when old, they will not swerve from it. Proverbs 22:6

Danny who possessed an insatiable appetite affiliated himself with the Knights of the Round Table. In addition to his passion for food he thirsted for intellectual challenges and competitive athletics. He found the right combination at Catholic Memorial High School in West Roxbury, MA. Although he was not 'round in physique he was always 'round food in an intellectual environment akin to the 'coffee houses' of old. Thankfully, Catholic Memorial satisfied he quest for sustenance.

Like most student-athletes, Danny was coachable: he took instruction well, and he accepted correction. Whether in the classroom, athletic field, or the hockey rink he was determined to master the skills necessary for success. His natural stubbornness enabled him to persevere, but it was his insight that made him so valuable for teammates and classmates alike.

Danny loved physical activity, playing more than a half-dozen sports intensely over the years, and along the way he was blessed with outstanding coaches. A good coach makes a great difference in the world, not just guiding the athletic development of the young people entrusted to him, but also becoming a mentor who instills lifelong lessons about fairness, duty, intention, and consequence. Under the tutelage of such good men Danny developed confidence and courage. Sports also enabled him to express as well as to confine his redheaded temper.

While in the eighth grade, our son Jack recalls visiting Boston College High School (BC High) as a prospective student. The BC High soccer coach's presentation consisted of a video of a soccer game against Catholic Memorial High School (CM), Danny's high school. On the video, Jackie immediately spotted Danny playing like an enraged tiger, subsequently cited with a yellow card for rough play. Jack quickly spoke out and said, "That's my brother" and hastened to assure the BC High coach that, "I don't play as rough as he does." "That's too bad," replied the coach. "He's exactly the type of player I want at BC High!"

Experiencing both victory and defeat in sports taught all of our children to enjoy rivalry without rancor, and to win and lose with grace. Self-control is a lot to ask of any young person, but spending hours in the give and take of a game trains them well. For Danny, of course, the athletic experience was augmented by periods of reflection, in the penalty box.

Catholic Memorial's Silver Knight

God was with the boy as he grew up. (Genesis 21:20a)

Danny went from eighth grade at St. Joseph's School in Needham to Catholic Memorial High School in West Roxbury, a five-minute commute via commuter rail. CM is administered by the Irish Christian Brothers, whose reputation for no-nonsense discipline with a strong Catholic reputation appealed to Danny. We thought it fortuitous at the time when Jack chose to attend BC High in Dorchester, a forty-five minute commute via commuter rail, that there would be fewer fights and increased harmony at home. Given that the BC High Eagles and CM Silver Knights are archrivals, however, domestic tranquility was short lived as sharp jibes quickly returned to our family dinner table.

Summers brought a respite, however, when Father Leo (Papa Leo) Pollard, SJ, former longtime BC High Hockey Coach invited Danny to join Jack on an elite summer hockey team that he coached and played games at the Pilgrim Area in Hingham, a town south of Boston he was delighted. A 'Silver Knight' from Catholic Memorial High School was the center-iceman on an 'Eagle" team comprised of BC High players. Danny was thrilled to skate for such a highly regarded coach, even though he was the sole Silver Knight amongst *Les Aigles* (the Eagles).

Typically for Danny, he and Papa Leo became good friends, which gave Danny a new way to provoke Jack. Whenever Danny spotted Papa Leo at a BC–CM game, he rushed over to greet him and warmly shake his hand. Naturally the Eagles booed the interloper furiously. Worst of all — or best, from Danny's point of view — were the football games when Danny was suited up as the Silver Knight Mascot. He would prolong his greetings and handshake on the BC High side of the field because he truly enjoyed Father Pollard; and, an ancillary benefit was that his presence aggravated the Eagles and their fans.

Dan Kennedy was the Knight mascot in 1992, and 15 years later he was still defending CM against the BC High Eagle.

Danny and Jack shared a love of ice hockey, and, while in high school, both were certified by the American Hockey Association of the United States (AHAUS) as Referees. Consequently, they would referee Youth Hockey Games in the Boston area every weekend. Refereeing became a welcomed source of income as well as a way to further indulge their pleasure in the sport.

Sports, activities, and academics kept Danny busy at Catholic Memorial. Still aspiring to Notre Dame's Golden Dome, he challenged himself to excel, and he grew steadily in faith, knowledge, and leadership, motivated by the faculty to "be all that God wants you to be." Danny frequently quoted his math teacher, Brother Joseph Heeran, CPC: "Always remember; hard work plus enthusiasm equal success and, most importantly, you must have *desire!*"

Brother Heeran possessed a strong Bostonian accent (dropping 'r's' with regularity) which intrigued Danny who subsequently became enthralled with accents and quickly became a masterful impersonator. His ability to imitate accents enhanced and authenticated his storytelling which captivated the listener.

I don't know whether the delivery of Brother's Heeran's message was more important than the content of the message but Danny learned to appreciate that both 'delivery and content' were essential in capturing the attention of a listener. Whether it was style or not he definitely grasped the message.

Desire, hard work and *enthusiasm* became the watchwords which defined his high school years, as he strived to be the best in every sphere. In addition to being elected as President of the Forensics team and President of the National Honor Society, he was also awarded a scholarship for mathematics and, he lettered in hockey, tennis, soccer, and track. In addition to these extra-curricular activities he added more to his plate; he joined the Drama Club and participated in the annual school play.

In his junior year he was cast in the role of the affable Leonard Vole who was tried for murder in a play based on Agatha Christi's short story, Witness for the Prosecution. He was a natural for that role and he thoroughly enjoyed the endless rehearsals and of course, the performances to a packed auditorium.

Danny especially loved the debating and speech contests, and he became a strong public speaker. Natural talent plus hard practice added up to statewide recognition in the Massachusetts Secondary School Oratorical Contest and the National Forensic Finals in Chicago, Ill. There, never one to waste an opportunity, Danny somehow squeezed in a Chicago Cubs game at Wrigley Field.

In high school Danny decided he was now too old to continue as an Altar Server at St. Joseph, so he offered to become a weekend lector. As the youngest lector in the parish he was conspicuous. He possessed a fine speaking voice, enunciated well and exhibited considerable confidence. The parishioners were impressed and sought to have other young people read or cantor. Bishop Roberto Gonzalez officiated at his Confirmation; Danny served as the lector and selected Patrick as his Confirmation name. He felt he was honoring his paternal grandfather as well as the patron saint of the Archdiocese of Boston and he was proud to be known as Daniel Joseph Patrick Kennedy!

In 1992, at age 18, he had the honor of reading at St. Joseph's 75th Anniversary Celebratory Mass. He was also designated as one of the parishioners to contribute an essay in the Commemorative Book. He was delighted to represent the high school students of

St Joseph's parish. Even after Danny matriculated to Providence College he continued to be active the parish life of the Church of St. Joseph in Needham.

Everything didn't break his way in 1991; Bill Hanson, CM's hockey coach, made the difficult decision to cut one of his wings at the start of his senior year. "Okay, Coach," was Danny's quick comeback, "I'll be the manager." That CM team was very strong as two players on it eventually played in the National Hockey League.

"It was like having another coach on the ice," Coach Hanson recalled. "He was terrific." Managers were allowed to dress for one game, and Danny selected the final game of the before the Super-Eight statewide Hockey Tournament. "The first thing he did was draw a penalty," his coach marveled. "Oh, he was a hard-nosed kid."

Danny was also capable of showing surprising maturity. "In our senior year at Catholic Memorial High School Dan persuaded me to attend college. He truly turned my life around. I will be forever grateful." Those words were written sixteen years later by Police Lieutenant Mark Leitner, of the Watertown, MA Police Department who brought his children forward to be blessed after Danny's First Mass. Lieutenant Leitner carries Danny's Prayer Card, next to the Miranda Warning Card, in his wallet. The prayer card was also with him on the night he donned his bulletproof vest when the Watertown Police Force apprehended the Boston Marathon Bombers. "His wisdom at seventeen years of age speaks volumes about his character and interest in others" said Lieutenant Leitner.

Every senior aspiring to go to college is confronted with a decision; they must determine to which college they should apply. Danny's mind was made up long ago. Given his high grades, exceptional SAT scores, his extracurricular activities and he leadership qualities, his academic advisors felt confident about his chances of being accepted at the University of Notre Dame. Our Pastor, Father Jim Haddad wrote a strong letter of recommendation on his behalf assuring Danny that his impeccable credentials exceeded any other applicant he had previously recommended to the University of Notre Dame and all had been accepted.

Danny was excited during the application process and he proudly produced the essay he intended to submit to the University of Notre Dame. When Alice read the essay she said; "You will never be admitted after the Admissions Department reads this essay." He was perplexed with Alice's remark and asked why she was so negative. She responded; "no one will want to read whether or not you were tormented by your sisters, you should have chosen a better topic".

At the time, the rejection rate at Notre Dame was at least 75 percent and, the university was deliberately striving to accept more women than men. With that in mind a red flag may have gone up in the Admissions Office when Danny's essay was read. The topic of confrontation with sisters would not square with the university's selection strategy. Whatever the reason, Danny's application was rejected. Danny was devastated, as was Father Haddad who thought it was a 'slam-dunk'. Note Bene; Father Haddad did not read the essay!

Deep indeed is the wisdom of the maternal heart!

Notre Dame's rejection letter hit him like a physical blow, but it was Danny's nature to forge ahead, find an opening, and shoot for the goal. He swallowed his disappointment and shifted his focus to Providence College in Rhode Island, where several Catholic Memorial classmates were enrolling. One was his close friend Mike Rush, who similar to Danny, was unabashedly Catholic and enjoyed serving the Church. One obvious positive stood out for me: Providence was 30 miles away versus the grueling 800 to South Bend.

Upon graduation from Catholic Memorial High School, he was presented with the prestigious Stephen R. Power Community Service Award. In 1992, Danny also was selected as the first recipient of the Robert Baggett Memorial Scholarship which had been established by a local Anheuser Busch Beverage Distributorship; Quality Beverage of Taunton, MA. This honor was not only remuneratively welcomed but it also led to a summer job! The executives at the distributorship were so impressed with Danny's high school credentials they offered him summer employment during his four years at Providence College.

His responsibilities included operating a corporate to visit various clients in order to repair malfunctioning equipment. In essence he was dispatched to unclog beer lines at various establishments all along Boston's South Shore, including Foxboro Stadium, home of the National Football League's New England Patriots. Danny enjoyed the work, especially when the distributorship was seeking to find someone to don the Bud Man costume at group promotional events. As the former Silver Knight mascot at Catholic Memorial he assured them that he had the required experience.

As he assumed his additional role as 'Bud Man' he filled the corporate van with inflatable props to be used during the promotional demonstrations.

Cheerfully abusing his access to the props, Danny once installed a 40-foot inflatable Budweiser beer can on our front lawn — then pretended surprise when I demanded its immediate removal. Well-aimed teasing and outlandish practical jokes were among the many talents he took with him to Providence College, sometimes to the Dominicans' chagrin.

Looking back, Danny saw the readjustment in his undergraduate aspiration as providential, for the Dominican influence was to prove powerful in his spiritual growth. Providence was where — in the midst of a social whirl, academic rigor, community service, and a stint as The Friar mascot — Danny began seriously contemplating a religious calling. I don't know whether Papa Leo Pollard ever spoke to Danny directly, but he did tell me during Danny's senior year at CM that he hoped Danny would become a Jesuit — or even a Dominican, "just as long as he becomes a priest!" First the Mite hockey coach in Westfield, then the wife of the Mite hockey coach in Needham and now the former BC High hockey coach all noting a spiritual dimension in Danny. Interesting!

PART TWO: DAN THE MAN

Chapter 4: Home Away From Home

Providence College's Part-Time Friar

So we are ambassadors for Christ.
(2 Corinthians 5:20a)

Going away to college is a big step for anyone but it was clear that Danny was up for this great adventure. On freshman move-in day he stuffed our car with everything deemed necessary for college life in 1992: sporting gear, electronics, snacks, more sports gear, more gadgets — and perhaps a few pens and notebooks. Once we parked at Fennell Hall, the two made countless trips to the 4th floor; dashing up and down the stairs as we lugged his bags and boxes to his room, while I was grimacing, he was grinning from ear to ear.

Suddenly it was time to say good-bye. Alice was stoic; Danny was excited to start making friends; and I, true to form, supplied the tears. I cried not just because Danny inflicted one of his deliberately bone-crushing handshakes in farewell. I cried because I felt a loss.

For years Danny had been my enthusiastic companion at baseball games, football games, and hockey games, driving to and from countless practices and meets, cheering for our teams on television whatever the sport, and kneeling beside me at Mass more times than I could count. Would all be well for our young man? I prayed it would be, and sure enough, when Danny returned for Thanksgiving he couldn't stop telling us story after story of campus life and the fun he was having. Anyone could see how happy he was at Providence College.

From the beginning Danny felt right at home in the Catholic community of Providence College. He plunged into his studies and eagerly became active in campus organizations, including long distance running. I don't know what motivated him but he immediately volunteered to help in the chaplain's office. It wasn't long before he applied for membership in the student service organization, the prestigious Friars Club. Upperclassmen promptly voted the redhead from Needham into the Friars Club of Providence College.

The Friars Club's mission of Christian service suited Danny perfectly. Members conduct campus tours for prospective students, tutor other students, visit local nursing homes, assist the college administration with campus activities, and contribute service hours to benefit the wider community. Danny, who had always been a bit of a clotheshorse, felt proud to wear the club uniform in the school colors: a natty white blazer and jet-black tie.

Mike Rush, Danny's high school pal, also joined the Friars Club, as did Mike Cuddy, another chaplain's assistant and soon to be a good friend. Later Mike Cuddy began seminary formation with the Dominicans, and he, Father James M. Cuddy, OP was ordained one week before Father Dan. The two had much in common.

Have I mentioned his rapid stride? It was obvious from his gait that he had a purpose in life, a mission to accomplish, whatever that may be. One day, shortly after matriculating to PC as he was striding across campus Danny was greeted by one of the white-robed Dominican Friars. Although he didn't know at the time the friar was the college president, Father John Cunningham, OP; the two of them began to chat. What sports did Danny follow? All of them, said Danny, and Father Cunningham promptly offered his

mid-court seats at the Providence Civic Center for any home basketball games he was unable to attend (a frequent occupational
hazard for college presidents). The offer was not without a proviso
as Father Cunningham proceeded to state; "I realize you are a redhead," Father Cunningham continued, "so I want you to know I will
not tolerate any fights if you occupy my seats."

Danny was thrilled. On campus only a few weeks and he had
been offered the presidential seats at the Civic Center. I imagine
Father Cunningham knew perfectly well the character of the freshman he had stopped. Danny's application had been stellar — and
his red hair was hard to miss.

Father Cunningham trusted Danny enough to have him pick
up college guests at the airport or train station in the presidential
car. Only once did Danny make the mistake of turning in the car
with the radio set at full blast to his favorite station; the president
delivered a scolding — and a music critique.

Early in Danny's freshman year Brother Kevin O'Connell, OP,
the moderator of the Friars Club, urged him to take his First Degree in the Knights of Columbus campus council. The core principles of the Knights of Columbus, Charity, Unity, Fraternity and
Patriotism appealed to Danny, and before the end of the semester
he was a Third Degree member of Friar Council #5787. An enthusiastic advocate, Danny promoted membership to his peers at
Providence and even traveled to other colleges to help establish
collegiate Councils.

As in high school, Danny's peers soon recognized his leadership abilities. His good nature and friendliness won him many
friends, and even when he heard a contrary opinion about a favorite sports team or a differing point of view, he handled it adroitly.
He had an in-depth knowledge on many topics and could skillfully

prod the other person with purportedly innocuous questions which precipitated a response that placed the other person in a defensive mode. People admire people who pleasantly and persuasively engage in discussions. To me, his popularity was no surprise as Danny genuinely liked people. After all, he had been cultivating friendships with our elderly neighbors and parishioners all his life. It also helped that he was not adverse to self-deprecating remarks, aka making a spectacle of himself. He would do anything, anything at all, for a good laugh. I think he truly believed that God wants us to enjoy life and he did, enjoy life.

Unlike those who like to stereotype others, Danny was genuinely interested in everyone he met as an individual. He believed everyone has a unique point of view, and he used small talk just to break the ice and establish a common ground so he could move on to the deeper levels of conversation he enjoyed most.

Long before formally studying ministerial techniques, Danny had figured out for himself how to prepare the ground for fruitful conversations — and sometimes even *conversions*. It was his habit to listen closely, ask questions to clarify, and then suggest ideas to prompt further reflection. Should Danny have a differing opinion that he wanted to share — as was often the case with which he was passionate — his prior attentiveness would have earned him a fair hearing. It was a mix of courtesy and strategy that seldom failed to hits its mark.

On August 19, 1993, Danny's maternal grandmother, Alice Haggerty, died. It was meaningful to me in that he answered the phone call and he was the first to know that 'Nana' just died. The reason that was meaningful is that, upon hearing the news, he immediately bolted down the stairs and out the front door. As I discovered later, his reaction though highly unusual, had absolutely nothing to do with grief. A few months prior to the phone call he realized that his Catholic Memorial High School Ring was missing and, per usual, he accused his sisters of taking his ring, and again, per usual, they denied any involvement. His fruitless search went on for weeks and eventually the topic appeared to be a forgotten incident.

For some reason the news of Nana's passing prompted him to rush out of the house, into the garage, climb into the attic and... find his Catholic Memorial Ring. He found it in a cardboard box just where 'he' had left the ring. I thought it was 'interesting' that his memory would be jogged by receiving news of Nana's death, the same person who, to Alice surprise and, to my surprise, stated several years earlier that she thought Danny would be a priest. Years later, after he was ordained, I have come to believe that Nana must have been more fortuitous in recognizing signs of vocation than we were when several years earlier she asked, 'Danny is going to be a priest isn't he?'

Deep indeed is the wisdom of the maternal heart.

Even though Danny was in a preparation mode for his rapidly approaching sophomore year at Providence College he sat down and composed a remembrance of Nana. His tribute, which he read at the end of her Funeral Mass, elicited smiles and tears even from those who knew her as well as those who barely knew her. The appreciative, respectful, sweetly humorous recollections showed a gentleness, insight, and faith that took many in our extended family by surprise. Nana's grandchildren generally knew Danny best as a redheaded jock always ready for a joke at family picnics. But in the face of death and eternity a new side of that rowdy boy was exposed. It gave everyone pause.

Another mascot joined Danny's repertoire as he commenced his sophomore year at Providence College; he donned The Friar costume for the collegiate basketball season. Fans at the Big East Tournament held at Madison Square Garden witnessed the PC Friar sparring with the Villanova University Wildcat, deploying his best Bud Man charges and Silver Knight feints. Dr. Joe Ciccone remembers the time he decided switch costumes and he make an appearance as the Anheuser-Busch 'Bud Man'. He strolled into Dr. Joe's off-campus digs at the College of the Holy Cross, bearing a keg and brandishing a sign: "Bud Man Salutes the Guys at 547 Cambridge Street."

Father Joseph Barranger, OP, Providence College Chaplain for Students when Danny was an undergraduate later wrote, "I remember Danny as a college kid, his laughter, and his love for life, his crazy pranks, and his constant mischievousness, all of which brought joy to my life and were part of what would eventually make him a great young priest. I also know he was an enthusiastic cheerleader for vocations."

Which came first: the Silver Knight, the Bud Man, the Friar, or the vocations cheerleader? Father Barranger saw Danny in action on campus, and had no doubt the Man Behind the Mask was a future priest.

As an added responsibility Danny was designated as First Assistant to the Dominican priest charged with organizing all major on-campus functions, from parent weekends to alumni events and graduation week. The Administrator was a demanding taskmaster who loaded his aides with duties and demanded excellent results, and his helpers were prone to swift burnout. Danny proved the exception. Though only a sophomore, he was personable, efficient, organized, and reliable; consequently, he served three years as First Assistant. The many organizational skills he honed in that role were later tapped by his corporate employers and the Archdiocese of Boston.

Among his annual Commencement duties were escorting and catering to the prestigious honorary degree recipients, which generally included airport chauffeuring. Danny accompanied Jane Pauley, then anchor of NBC's *Today* Show; Dr. Dolores Grier, founder of the Association of Black Catholics Against Abortion and later Vice Chancellor of the Archdiocese of New York; a noted Brazilian cardinal; as well as a PC alum, Raymond L. Flynn, Mayor of the City of Boston and future United States Ambassador to the Vatican.

Danny was also selected to assume the role of a Providence College Ambassador, whose charge is to reflect the teachings of Saints Dominic and Thomas Aquinas in a genuine and enthusiastic manner to campus visitors and guests. Danny was determined to present an enthusiastic and positive image of Providence College. That sense of purpose — helping his Catholic community shine in the eyes of the world — closely reflected how his personal goals were developing. His contagious laughter was the spillover of his deep joy for life, which came from his ever-growing sense of God's love.

Equivocation or hesitation was never apparent in Danny's psyche. If he could act to solve a problem, he did so post haste. He was direct in dealing with every situation. As a junior, when Danny learned that a sophomore friend had failed for the second time to be accepted into the Friars Club, Danny searched the campus until he found him; then he promised he would ensure acceptance next year if his friend would persevere and reapply. To this day his younger friend remembers that act of swift intervention as kindness incarnate.

I was active in various ministries at St. Anthony's Shrine on Arch Street in heart of downtown Boston. To Bostonians, the shrine was affectionately known as 'Arch Street' when the boys were in college I always invited Danny and Jackie to join me at the Annual Franciscan Golf Tournament. It was an enjoyable opportunity for people to 'meet and greet' the Friars informally. I also saw the event as an opportunity to bond with both sons and to introduce them to a few of my Franciscan Friar friends.

Danny seemed to click with several Franciscan Friars but he really connected with Father Fergus Healey, ofm who was an avid golfer. Father Fergus was joyful and upbeat and he was highly regarded in the Boston area as a deep and spiritual man. He was in awe of the distance of Danny and Jackie's tee shots and looked forward to seeing them every year. After an arduous day on the golf course it wasn't unusual to see Danny and Father Fergus engaged in a deep conversation at the Awards Dinner.

As a senior, when he heard that a freshman friend was considering transferring, Danny arranged a meeting with the Dominican Dean of Student Life. The young man's problems were resolved, and he became an active member of the college community. Later his two younger brothers also found success at Providence.

Many high school classmates were with Danny at Providence College, and the gang stayed connected. He told an interviewer from Catholic Memorial some years later, The by-word on campus was, "you can be certain to find the CM boys in two places: the party on Saturday night and Mass on Sunday morning."

Somehow Danny managed to blend frequent social outings with a strong spiritual commitment. The winter immediately preceding graduation, Danny wrapped up a night out with friends by ducking into Aquinas Chapel for a brief period of Eucharistic Adoration. When he noticed that another student in the chapel was crying, Danny immediately asked if he could help. The young man explained that he was distraught because the Pastor of his parish in Quincy, MA, Father Cornelius Heery had suddenly died. Danny promised that he too would offer prayers for Father Heery. The student's deep admiration for his deceased pastor, precipitating a visit to the Eucharist in the middle of the night, in utter sorrow, to pray for him — impressed Danny deeply. He knew losing a family member or a close friend is terribly sad, now he began to realize that losing a priest is a blow to the entire Church.

Everyone who knew Danny wondered what path he would travel after college, and some thought his spiritual maturity should incline him toward priesthood. He had dated the same girl all four years at Providence, and her mother once told him straight out, "If

it weren't for my daughter you would probably become a priest."
On the other hand, a classmate who had known him since childhood pointed out what happened one year at a college reunion.
Marguerite Cail recalled, "When Danny told everyone he had just
entered the seminary, they thought it was another joke!"

Father Joseph Barranger, Providence College Chaplain during
Danny's years at PC kept in touch with him after graduation because, as he later wrote, "I noted Dan's faithfulness to Mass, his
tireless defense of the Faith (which won him a few enemies). I perceived an interior searching and yearning that raised the possibility
of a vocation." Eventually Father Barranger became Danny's Spiritual Director, advising him and guiding him during what would
prove to be a long, long journey to discernment of his vocation.

Father Barranger (L) and Father Cuddy (R) with Danny

A month before graduating as a business major, Danny received a 'dream job' offer from a renowned international consulting corporation to become a software analyst. This unparalleled

opportunity would expose him to the best business practices of a top-notch firm with ample opportunity for rapid advancement.

Danny never let hesitancy enter his thought process; identify the problem determine the course of action and, full steam ahead. He accepted the offer. After serving as a college ambassador, he felt ready and eager to become an ambassador for the corporate world. He joked that this mascot would be not Bud Man, a Silver Knight or, even a Friar but "a suit." For someone who loved challenges and prided himself on being nattily dressed in the latest style clothing, the road ahead looked exciting!

Chapter 5: Like Mother, Like Son

The woman who fears the Lord is to be praised.
(Proverbs 31:31)

When I consider my wife Alice's temperament and talents, there is no doubt where Danny acquired his gifts. They didn't emanate from the 'old man'.

On June 13, 1969, six months pregnant, the Assistant Manager of Carborundum Corporation's Massachusetts plant in West Springfield resigned her position to prepare for her true lifelong vocation: motherhood. As with everything she undertook, from repairing automobiles to remedying plumbing issues to solving mathematical problems or from playing golf to arranging parties Alice was 100% committed. Becoming a mother was a challenge she anxiously anticipated and achieved her objective. Commencing three months later she became a remarkable mother for all five of our high octane, 'spirited' children.

Looking back, I can only marvel at her abilities. Can you imagine the sheer logistical challenge of daily duties such as laundry, hygiene, dressing and feeding five children for every given event, in season and out of season? Alice also chauffeured them to doctor and dentist appointments, sports practices, soccer games and music lessons. Yet Alice pulled it off with boundless energy and never a complaint.

Aside from working for a living, I had one crucial task: follow her orders. At Alice's direction I took my place in the rotation — driving, tutoring, or coaching as needed. Frankly, it was not until

I assumed housekeeping chores in recent years that it began to register how hard she had worked to keep our home a welcoming place for friends, family, and an endless stream of visitors.

In addition to her organizational skills, Alice had the gift of understanding. This too was part of her legacy to Danny. When, as an adult, Katie described Danny the words she used could just as well have been applied to her mother:

"He was fair and could quickly assess a situation. He was a 'matter of fact' type guy and once he formulated his position he expressed it quickly and unequivocally. He was always easy to be around, funny-on-purpose and— most of all — he backed me up and challenged me at the same time. He listened intently, and seemed to appreciate my input. He validated me."

Whether the kids had woes to lament or triumphs to trumpet, she always made time to listen and was careful to treat each child individually. She encouraged all of them to make the most of their gifts, encouraging them and pointing out areas that required addition work. Alice's high expectations and steady support helped made each child eager to aspire for success — but if any outsider praised them, she invariably waved it off with a dismissive "They're just normal." She inculcated in each of the five that they were nothing special, they were 'just normal'. Alice disseminated extraordinary maternal advice. Another tenet in her instructional messages was her edict to look people in the eye, introduce yourself, and to address them by name prefaced by Mr. or Mrs. There were occasions when one of the kids would come and tell Alice that 'Sally' is such a nice lady. Alice confronted them with; "Sally? Don't you mean Mrs. Dempsey?" The response was 'she' encouraged them to call her 'Sally'. Alice responded, regardless of what 'Mrs.

Dempsey' may have said to you, her name is "Mrs. Dempsey" and that is the way you are to address her.

Alice's demeanor was mindful of the admonition in Luke 12:48: *"From everyone who has been given much, much will be demanded; and from the one who has been entrusted with much, much more will be asked."* Alice and I expected much from our children because they had been given much; health, home, a loving family and, they were being raised in the Catholic environment. On the flip side, God clearly expected much from Alice and I so we willingly accepted whatever wrinkles came into our daily life. Our 'apprentice adults' certainly kept us on our toes and, on our knees.

For years, Alice and the children spent summers in Dennisport, MA on Cape Cod. The kids and Alice all had summer occupations. Alice was the Property Manager of Dennis Seashores, a large complex of over (30), individually owned, cottages fronting on Nantucket Sound. In addition to hiring a competent staff Alice was always multi-tasking. If there was a guest in need of emergency first aid, she was available with her first aid kit, if there was a plumbing issue she had her pipe wrench, and if it was a carpentry issue she had her hammer and screwdrivers. Alice was also skilled in persuading penurious owners to replace refrigerators and stoves so that the guests would receive VIP treatment that would hopefully entice them to register for the following season.

At this charming beachside resort our children grew up sharing their mother's love for the ocean. Cape Cod was not a lazy vacation, however. She always encouraged them to keep busy, whether fishing, swimming, clamming, or flying kites, and anyone old enough to work was expected to find a summer job or two.

At age ten Danny obtained his first job; he donned a Boston Globe apron and began selling newspapers near a popular restaurant and, at church on Sundays. At eleven he was working full-time at a prominent restaurant, cleaning the greasy frying vats. It was a filthy job, but Danny loved making money, and also he kept up his side job of mowing lawns for Alice at Dennis Seashore Resort.

Every Friday evening I would arrive at the Cape, ready for a weekend of fun with my family. Would we be flying kites, or golfing, or sailing, or swimming? Whatever the kids proposed was my pleasure. To spare Alice kitchen chores I liked taking the family out to eat. This particularly delighted Danny, whose high activity level made him a bottomless pit.

During the weekend I graded the children's weekly essays, where each reported on at least one of that week's activities. When I sat down for the 'Reading of the Reports' it was with much anticipation.

One of Danny's reports began on a positive note:

"My week began on Sunday morning, I sold thirty-five copies of the Boston Globe and when I finished I went to Mass at Holy Trinity. On Monday morning I sold twenty-five copies of the Boston Globe. On Monday afternoon I made a deal with Mom. The deal was that when I banked $50 she would allow me to buy a plastic Sunfish."

Terrific! I was proud of Danny's exhibition of money management and long-range planning. A sunfish is a small sailboat, sturdy, easy to rig and maintain, perfect for a beginning sailor to handle, fairly inexpensive, and sure to hold up for many summers to come.

Did this foretell his future? In time; would he become a sailor? Would he join the United States Navy?

As I proceeded to read further, Danny's resourcefulness aka deviousness emerged:

> *"Mom thought it would take a while for me to save the money. She did not realize that I had $34 upstairs ready for the bank. On Tuesday morning I sold twenty-five papers and on Tuesday afternoon I bought a one-man boat!"*

Frankly, I admired his resourcefulness, while purportedly disapproving his deception in failing to divulge his hoard of money with Alice. Parenting is often a juggling act, scolding sternly while suppressing a smile.

There were however occasional confrontations; generally my response to brewing hostilities was 'work it out' or 'I don't wear a striped shirt, I am not a referee'! All of our kids were competitive but Danny and Jackie were extremely competitive. One Mother's day, the pressure cooker exploded; Danny and Jackie had a fistfight on our front lawn and Alice was visibly disturbed. Before I could reach them she had grasped both of them by their necks and shipped them off to separate rooms. Another trying incident occurred when they were teenagers, the day Danny received his driver's license. Big brother offered to chauffer Jackie on a short ride around town. When they returned from an abbreviated 'first ride' the two of them were punching each other in the front seat of the car! Alice told them to cease and desist but they ignored her plea for peace.

Always one to fight fire with fire, literally Alice swung into action. With her ever-ready toolbox close at hand she grabbed the hammer and immediately smashed the windshield. Glass splinters flew all over both boys as they cowered in the front seat. Armistice achieved! The boys sheepishly exited the car and she meted out appropriate punishment. Driver's license confiscated and Jackie's impending driving lessons canceled.

At times, parental guidance precipitates an unreceptive response culminating in a stressful situation; not with Alice and Danny. They had so much in common, their interests dovetailed on almost every aspect of life. Both possessed tremendous energy, abundant kindness and cheerful dispositions. Alice loved practical jokes, a brand of humor that Danny inherited. To their mutual delight, both loved hockey, clamming, flying kites, and maintaining cars. Bright, quick thinkers, they spoke their minds with confidence and loved to make others laugh.

For years both of them waxed their cars together, compared toolboxes, and happily vied for the latest gadgets. Even their strides matched: a swift, far-reaching gait that quickly left the rest of the world behind.

As Danny grew older he kept his frugal habits, yet managed to justify whatever made his work easier, proudly showing off his first cell phone, first Palm Pilot, first thumb drive, and so on. Alice always shared his delight in acquiring kits — clever, neatly packaged collections that supposedly simplified his life wherever he went, like his shoeshine kit, toiletry kit, pumpkin carving kit, and tailgate grilling kit. Ultimately, I think their hands-down favorite was the Mass kit that he used after his ordination.

Danny, like Alice, enjoyed helping people, particularly the elderly and needy. Once when Danny was in the 'working world' he told us that he gave a ten-dollar bill to a homeless man; good that his corporate paycheck allowed him to be that generous. Alice's penurious nature surfaced and she retorted; "a fiver would have been sufficient." She never met a dime she could not stretch.

Find a coin…give that to them, for me
and for you. (Matthew 17:27)

Our children had a mother who knew well what they were up to — for better and for worse — and who prayed for each child's particular needs every day. She attended Mass on First Fridays, led grace at the table when I was not there, and before retiring each night always prayed with the silver Rosary Beads engraved, 'Alice Marie Haggerty on the occasion of your First Holy Communion', that she received as a gift from her godfather, Melvin O'Leary. Alice was private about her faith, but Danny knew well that she kept her rosary close at hand every night, and I have no doubt his love for Alice paved the way for his love of the Blessed Mother.

Father Jim DiPerri observed, "Father Dan always sought balance in his life. Yes, laughter was an integral part of his persona and physical conditioning essential, but he gained spiritual strength from Jesus in the Blessed Sacrament. Dan also realized he needed to stay close to Jesus and to His Blessed Mother that was first and foremost in his mind".

As a priest, Father Dan showed deep devotion to the Blessed Mother. He often advised *sorrowful, confused,* or even *angry people* to visit a church, sit in front of the tabernacle, and *ask the Blessed Mother for her help.* He once told his sister Katie what he told them: "The Blessed Mother will never fail to come to help you. You can take that to the bank!" Another time he assured Katie to pray to Mary because "she works!" I hear echoes of Alice in both of those remarks.

In his First Mass of Thanksgiving as a newly ordained priest, Father Dan extended his appreciation to so many who had encouraged him on his 'path to priesthood' and stressed their importance as he struggled to discern what God wanted him to do with his life.

"My prayer today is that I never lose sight of the powerful Christian witness that I first saw in my parents and in my siblings," he said. "This powerful Christian witness is what I was taught to look for in friends, and I certainly have found it."

Danny grew up with a multitude of friends, but first and foremost he grew up in the rough of tumble of his own family, with his brother and three sisters, and under his mother's watchful, loving eye. As they grew older, each son and daughter came to see Alice anew. She was no longer just Mommy that whirlwind and dynamo we all took for granted for so many years. She was actually the embodiment of the "honorable woman" celebrated in Proverbs 31 for her uncomplaining, generous service to all those around her.

"Her children rise up and call her blessed; her husband, too, praises her:

'Many are the women of proven worth, but you have excelled them all.'"

As I write this Alice is bearing the cross of Alzheimer's disease. Each evening I feed her supper, and if it's a good night for her, we have a little sing-song together, enjoying the old favorites that linger in her memory. Much else is gone, but her natural cheerfulness and a brilliant smile occasionally occur and when they do it is like hitting a home run.

Every so often God provides us a moment of lucidity or levity which I construe as a spiritual 'pat on the back'. Recently, in order to elicit a smile, as I was feeding her and offering my customary suggestions — chew, swallow, drink, and so on — I said, "Alice, after all these years of giving instructions to this entire family, how does it feel to be taking orders from the family dummy?"

I wasn't certain whether my words would register but I was hoping for a facial expression of comprehension. Disappointingly for me, her vague expression did not change but then slowly, and deliberately she softly and hesitatingly enunciated, "its...*tough!*" I roared with laughter. I was thrilled. Somehow Alice had connected the wires in her mind and arrived at the correct conclusion. Ten years earlier she would have arrived at the same conclusion but would have expressed herself much more vituperatively!

Soon enough Alice will be grinning again as she greets her beloved redheaded rascal. I can see the two of them striding side-by-side, mother and son, full-speed ahead, straight through the Gate of Heaven to God's loving embrace and unending joy.

Chapter 6: "Call Waiting!"

Unless the Lord builds the house, they labor in vain who build. (Psalm 127:1a)

Andersen Consulting (which was later renamed to Accenture), the world's largest management consulting organization, assigned Danny to their Pleasanton, California Training Center for intensive technology training in their PeopleSoft Division. PeopleSoft was a newly development technological method that would provide clients with a brand-new tool for managing personnel. Behavioral Science skills were a by-product of the newly developed program. Danny's responsibility would be to instruct client administrators in methods to systematically collect employee data pursuant to providing greater executive insight.

Bringing administrators up to speed was crucial in reducing the risk of losing talented employees or identifying ineffective workers. PeopleSoft was a 'win win' for both the employer and ambitious employees. Increased workforce efficiency and higher productivity were the goals shared by Andersen and its clients, and they became the focus of Danny's energies as well. Danny was all about winning and Andersen Consulting has a well-prepared script. He was sold on PeopleSoft's winning formula and anxious to put their plan into operation.

After the three month Training Program concluded, Danny made site visits to various Andersen clients, where Danny oversaw the installation and implementation of the PeopleSoft Program. Andersen Corporation leased apartments in the locality of their clients so their field staff would be housed in close proximity. The ancillary benefit for the field staff would be able time to explore the local domain.

Andersen's generous travel policy allowed the field staff to travel back to Boston on weekends. He was pleased that he would continue be in his customary seat at Foxboro Stadium (currently Gillette Stadium) New England Patriots football games. At his friends' tailgate parties he loved manning the grill, and over the next few years he expanded his grilling franchise to games at Boston College and even the University of Notre Dame in South Bend, ID, where his brother Jack was working on advanced degrees in law and business. Friends said that Danny never relinquished the tools of his tailgating trade except to spiral a pass 50 yards across the parking lot, just to prove that wearing a suit had not impaired his arm or his aim. An enjoyable weekend generally culminated with another win for the New England Patriots.

Danny loved to plan outings, and while working on site for a client in New Jersey, he organized a weekend trip with Jack and me. The three of us rendezvoused at the Baseball Hall of Fame in Cooperstown, New York. We wrapped up our father and son's weekend at the 10:30am Sunday Mass at St. Patrick's Cathedral in Manhattan, celebrated by John Cardinal O'Connor. Danny admired Cardinal O'Connor, who had been a chaplain in the U.S. Navy and who frequently spoke about his love for his parents, the priesthood, sports, and the Navy — often in that order.

Despite long workdays during his field assignments Danny managed to indulge his love of sports, training hard with long distance runs and beginning to think about taking on a marathon. At 5'11" and well muscled from hockey, he did not have a runner's physique, yet he felt certain his determination would alleviate that inadequacy. A bonus in developing a running program was, while it satisfied his need to be active and physically engaged it also released stress associated with his employment responsibilities. Running was a time devoted purely to muscle motion, breathing, and silence — elementals that enabled a time for spirituality, however exhausted his body might be.

He allowed adequate time to improving his golf game as well; ultimately lowered his handicap to 15. He would never match Jack's championship level of play, but his swing improved and, with his muscular build, his drives traveled a long distance.

"Danny was 22 years old at this time," his sister Katie recalls, "when landed the plum job that brought him to a place in New Jersey directly across the Hudson River from New York City. He enjoyed the freedom to travel, had sufficient money in his pocket, and a stipend for weekend travel — plus it was an opportunity for his sister to obtain a free flight to visit him!" Katie and Danny had great fun together. She vividly remembers touring San Francisco with him, even though he insisted on including a visit to Alcatraz.

Between work and play, Danny's life seemed to be full, or overfull, 24/7.

Danny managed to keep in touch with all of his old friends, some of whom were aware that he suspected a call to the priesthood. His college biology professor, Father Mark Nowel OP, answered a message from Danny in July 1997 by saying, "If you're not engaged by summer of 1999, I'm signing you up!" In Father Mark's mind, Danny's calling was obvious and his delay in addressing it signaled a lack of attention, not a lack of vocation.

Evidently he was contemplating Fr. Nowel's suggested but altering the timeframe. Katie recalls her visit with Danny in Manhattan which caught her off guard by announcing that if he had not met the girl of his dreams by the time he was thirty, he would enter the seminary. Was this one of his 'tongue in cheeks' remarks? Katie wondered. If he were serious, surely he wouldn't need eight years of lead-time.

But as they talked more about it, Katie realized that Danny was sincere. "I figured most childhood thoughts — like becoming a firefighter or professional hockey player — tend to pass when you graduate from college," she recalled, but clearly Danny's thoughts were roaming far beyond his corporate duties and downtime with his friends. In the midst of his busy life, her little brother was wrestling with internal, spiritual demands as well.

Our home in Needham was Danny's weekend base when he returned to Boston, but sometimes we barely saw him. He kept busy visiting friends, and he was often quiet — worn out, I figured — as I drove him to Logan Airport Sunday evenings for the return flight to wherever he was assigned that month. Unlike him, he was unduly quiet on those trips to Logan he always seemed to be deep in thought, seemingly reluctant to return to his apartment-of-the-month.

One Friday night Danny arrived home looking glum and he retired early. "Is he sick?" Alice wondered which precipitated my trip to the second floor to check on him. Danny opened his heart. "Dad," he said and then dejectedly, the story poured out.

He was exhausted, not physically but emotionally. The novelty of living out of a suitcase had worn thin months ago. Ending each day in a silent, impersonal, short-term apartment was dreary and depressing. He missed Boston. He missed his pals. In less than two years the thrill of his first professional job had evaporated, precipitating disillusion and disappointment.

Danny also mentioned being troubled by his conscience, because his work led directly to terminating employees. Yes, he understood that his clients' employees could now count on fair evaluations, unclouded by pettiness or bias. Yes, he appreciated that someone who was not a good fit would probably be happier moving elsewhere. Still, the thought of displaced workers and upended lives and families did not sit well. Thanks to Catholic Memorial High School and Providence College, Dan was well aware of Catholic social justice teachings, and the efficiency of his work seemed, at some level, ruthless and even inhumane.

Back to Beantown

Return home, each of you, for it is I who have brought this about. (1 Kings 12:24b)

An unexpected answer to Dan's discomfort arrived in the form of a headhunting offer from a global chemicals and minerals company, Cabot Corporation, headquartered in Massachusetts. Cabot wanted Danny to use his newly acquired skills as a human resources software analyst to implement modernization in their organization. Dan would be housed in Cabot's Billerica, MA office fifteen miles northwest of Boston. Travel requirements would be infrequent and the duration of which would be no longer than four or five days consisting of international treks, the prospect of which intrigued Danny. He was excited about the prospect of visiting Asia, South America and various European countries. With unabashed enthusiasm he accepted Cabot Corporation's offer.

Danny quickly settled back into his former stomping grounds. With a few friends he rented an apartment in Charlestown, one of Boston's oldest neighborhoods, which was located in the former Charlestown Navy Yard adjacent to the USS Constitution (Old Ironsides) the three-masted frigate named by George Washington and launched in 1787. He was domiciled a half-hour drive from Billerica — and east of Needham, where his boyhood bedroom was always waiting. Being so close to home, Danny happily rejoined our family parish in Needham, St. Joseph's. It wasn't long before he rejoined the parish lector team and he also signed up to teach Confraternity of Christian Doctrine (CCD).

Danny also renewed another familiar place to spend time; the nearby town of Natick. "Where have you been?" Alice would invariably ask, only to hear one cryptic word: "Natick." That was Danny's code word for the Perpetual Eucharistic Adoration Chapel of St. Patrick's Church, where he often spent some time. Somehow, despite his new job with Cabot and incessant social life, Danny was deliberately making room for adoration, spending time with Jesus Christ face to face. In spite of being a gregarious guy he was a private person especially when it came to his relationship with the Lord. He treasured a personal relationship with Christ...*when you pray, go to your inner room, close the door, and pray to your Father in secret. (Matthew 6:6-7)*

Years later, when he gave talks on vocations, Danny often described the power of Eucharistic Adoration in his life. During his first few years in Needham he attended First Friday Mass with his mother who was devoted to attending nine consecutive First Friday Masses. Actually Alice went well beyond 'nine'; her streak of First Fridays was endless. After Mass, Father Bob Hennessey placed the Eucharist in a Monstrance and placed it in the center of the Altar and he noted how intensely people responded:

"As I observed the people in church, one thing was clear: the object of everyone's gaze was no ordinary statue or icon; it was clearly something much more. It was the same Christ that was just offered in the Holy Sacrifice of the Mass. It seemed that everyone was just being 'still' before God."

As a young boy Danny began pondering the mystery of the Real Presence and discovered the blessed gift of silence — something lacking in most young people's plugged-in lives.

"Throughout my life I have sought refuge in the Eucharist," Dan wrote later in notes for a talk he would give to young Catholics. "As my awe and understanding of Christ's Presence matured through the years, the Eucharist has become therapeutic for me. In the quiet of an adoration chapel I knew that I could find stillness before the Lord." Undistracted and unresisting, he could open himself to divine grace.

Danny credited his time before the Eucharist as crucial to discerning his vocation:

"After college I poured myself into my work as a computer software consultant. My job required considerable travel; sometimes I worked eighty hours a week. In spite of those lengthy days, somehow I was able to escape the busyness of 'my world' and gather my thoughts with the help of Jesus, in Eucharistic Adoration. It was in these quiet moments that my vocation became clearer to me. As my vocation matured, Eucharistic Adoration became a central part of my life; it has been a wonderful discernment tool for me."

If Danny had one message to give young men, it was to kneel before the Eucharist and listen.

At Cabot Corporation Dan found a warm welcome from his new colleagues. A few were put off that he always declined to join them for lunch, but Danny felt no need to explain that he had a found a noon Mass to attend.

Brother Kevin O'Connell, the Friars Club chaplain at Providence College, was pleased that Danny had returned to Boston, for he believed Danny needed to give the seminary a try even if he was still unsure. Brother Kevin always invited Danny back to the Providence College campus for major Dominican Feast Days, during which Danny met other friends of the Dominicans who, like him, loved to be at St. Thomas Aquinas Friary. Being surrounded by the familiar white robes that had marked his college years evoked many happy memories, and Danny looked forward to these visits.

Providence College's former chaplain, Father Joseph Barranger, OP was assigned to St. Stephen's Priory in Dover, MA, south of Needham, enabling him to maintain contact with many former PC students in the Boston area. He kept an appraising eye on Danny, as he let me know during a luncheon convened to announce Mike Rush's candidacy for the Massachusetts House of Representatives.

Danny had been Mike's Campaign Manager in his previous successful presidential campaigns in high school and in college. Mike joked that he needed Danny around for good luck, thus Alice and I were both invited to the campaign kickoff.

At the luncheon Father Barranger, OP cornered me to ask, "When is Danny going to apply to St. John's Seminary?" I was taken aback when he told me some of Danny's closest friends were certain that he was considering the seminary. Father Barranger elaborated that a close friend, Jen Toto previously predicted that Mike Rush would resign his secondary school teaching position and enter politics, while Danny would ultimately become a priest.

Their certainty floored me. Danny never broached the subject with Alice or me. Would it help or hurt if I butted in and asked Danny where things stood? After considerable soul searching, I resolved not to violate Danny's privacy by mentioning Father Barranger's conversation with him. I decided to implement reverse psychology and say nothing that might be misconstrued instead I was determined to pray assiduously for his discernment of God's will.

Would I have loved to be kept in the loop? Absolutely. I was certain though that Danny would ultimately do the Lord's will no matter what was asked of him — and no matter what Alice or I might say. "Just speak louder, Lord," I prayed. Danny was still so busy racing around that I was concerned he might have trouble hearing.

Pilgrimage

Blessed the man who finds refuge in you, in their hearts are pilgrim roads.
(Psalm 84:6)

Dan's position at Cabot Corporation entailed traveling to South America, Europe, and Asia. Any Catholic who has traveled knows the joy of attending Mass in a foreign tongue, where the Church's universality can be seen, heard, and touched. Italy, with its wealth of holy sites, especially delighted Dan. On one of his business trips, Alice flew from Boston to Paris, met Dan and stayed with him in his first-class hotel. After his daily schedule of meetings Danny and Alice toured the City of Lights, taking in the Louvre, Notre-Dame Cathedral, and, especially precious to Alice, the tomb of St. Catherine Labouré at 140 Rue du Bac.

On another occasion, Dan boarded a train from Paris to Brussels, Belgium to visit with Father Francis E. Reilly. As a six year old, Danny attended Father Reilly's ordination in Springfield and, in his first assignment to St. Mary's Church in Westfield, it was Father Reilly who used to skate with our kids in our backyard ice rink. At that time, Father Fran was on loan to the American College of the Immaculate Conception Seminary in Louvain, as a Spiritual Advisor. He was pleased to offer Danny a tour of the seminary and the Brussels region. Their reunion in Belgium included miles of biking through towns and countryside visiting the sites of many World War II battles. Seeing a priest who so thoroughly loved life and who so loved his work in the vineyard of the Lord gave Danny more food for thought.

Whenever Danny was in Paris he attended Mass at Notre-Dame Cathedral. On one particular trip the Saturday afternoon Mass was so crowded he could barely find a seat; eventually he squeezed into the center of pew 15/20 rows from the Altar. When the procession began he realized why the nave of the church was so crowded; the beloved Archbishop of Paris, Jean-Marie Cardinal Lustiger, was to be the celebrant. Danny realized the celebrant was a cardinal but, at that time in his life, he was unaware that the celebrant was a convert from Judaism; the internationally acclaimed 'Jewish Cardinal' and a close confidant of Pope John Paul II.

To Danny's astonishment, after the conclusion of the Mass, when Cardinal Lustiger was processing back up the center aisle he suddenly stopped the procession and leaned into Danny's pew to speak to him. At Danny's puzzled look, Cardinal Lustiger quickly translated what he had said into English, asking, "Where are you from?" "Boston," Danny replied. With a deep, searching look, the cardinal said, "When you arrive back in Boston, visit the bishop at the seminary, and tell him that I sent you." With that the procession continued to the back of the cathedral. Danny became an instant celebrity to the people around him as they thought he knew the cardinal.

When Bishop Robert E. Barron, currently Auxiliary Bishop of the Archdiocese of Los Angeles, was studying at the Institute Catholique de Paris he met with Cardinal Lustiger. In a correspondence, I related Cardinal Lustiger's brief conversation with Danny Bishop Barron. In his response to me Father Barron informed me that Cardinal Lustiger was a Mystic!

You, or I might have complied with a world famous cardinal's tout de suite; not Danny. He allowed his busy life and, stubbornness to take the lead; it was several years later before he finally approached the Rector of St. John's Seminary in Boston.

When Danny was settled back in Massachusetts he was intrigued to learn that a group of people went, regularly, to a densely wooded area in Medway, Massachusetts, to pray the Rosary and the Chaplet of Divine Mercy. The site, just a half-hour drive southwest of Needham, over run with vegetation, was identified by a Venezuelan visionary, Maria Esperanza, as a future site of a retreat center. Maria, who many believe to be a Mystic, previously established a Shrine to Our Lady in Betania, Venezuela, and who was subsequently prompted to establish Betania II in the United States.

In a dream, Maria saw herself locating an abandoned farmhouse and discovering a buried rock with the face of Jesus. On a visit to Framingham, Massachusetts she identified the dilapidated farmhouse seen in her dream, on this densely wooded area in Medway, Massachusetts. After digging feverishly, next to the farmhouse, she found the buried rock she had seen in her dreams, with the Face of Jesus. Frequently, when Danny was in 'Natick' he would plod through the underbrush of the abandoned farmhouse to pray the Chaplet of Divine Mercy. On one of those visits he took a picture of the wooded underbrush. When the film was developed, in the center of the picture of dense underbrush was a clearly defined, *large open door* in the midst of what was total and thick vegetation. He had no explanation for the phenomenon, except as possibly supernatural intervention.   Food for thought?

Today, at 154 Summer Street in Medway, MA, on the site of what had been densely overgrown vegetation stands a beautiful and expansive Spiritual Life and Marian Retreat Center; Betania II. The Rock with the Face of Jesus is displayed in a case in the Retreat House.

The Chaplet of Divine Mercy Chaplet is itself like a doorway through which we draw nearer to Jesus Christ. In praying the chaplet, Danny could immerse his worldly cares in the sea of Divine Mercy. He could say with Saint Faustina those simple words: *"Jesus, I Trust in You."*

Saint Faustina's prayer was popularized by Saint John Paul II, who wrote that *"Mercy is love's second name."* I imagine that Danny felt like everyone who prays the Chaplet: aware of our faults; grateful for Christ's abundant Mercy and mindful that anyone bound by injustice, illness, or other miseries needs, and deserves, our compassion and mercy. Danny's lifelong instinct to help others, to show kindness, to defend the weak — all his best tendencies were reinforced by prayers like the Chaplet of Divine Mercy.

In February, the Annual Cardinal's Discernment Retreat for priestly vocations is held at St. John's Seminary. In February 1999, Danny informed Alice and me that he planned on attending the retreat. That entire weekend we prayed that he would find guidance and enlightenment. When he came into our bedroom on Sunday night to debrief us on the retreat, he obviously had been deeply moved by the spirituality of the retreat. Yet he looked relieved as he explained that, after extensive prayer and several conferences, he concurred with the consensus that it would be advisable for him to continue a preparatory period of prayer prior to submitting an application to St. John's Seminary.

Even though Alice and I were praying for an immediate resolution, as long as he was comfortable with that course of action, and he was, we enthusiastically endorsed his plan.

Since then I have learned more about vocations and, in some cases, the slow evolution; occasionally with peaks and valleys. A boy may be intrigued by the priest's pivotal role in the Mass and Sacraments, and then begin to picture himself in that role, only to commence to worry whether he is worthy of such a lofty role to play in the game of life. Layman? Priest? Either way he has to beg God to reveal His plan. Should he feel drawn toward the seminary, there remain years of preparation — and at every point *"the father of lies"* (John 8:44) is there to sow doubt and discouragement.

Danny, who was invariably confident and sure of himself, persevered, and after the Discernment Retreat we noticed a more intense seriousness of purpose. Danny attended follow-up meetings at St. John's Seminary; he continued to seek out daily Mass whether he was home or traveling and, "Natick" stayed in the rotation. In the midst of his busy schedule for Cabot and his ongoing fraternization with his friends Danny kept praying for the grace to know God's will. Putting his newly intensified search in office terms, he told his sister Katie bluntly, "You can't keep God on 'call-waiting' " He was well on his way to acquiescence.

Father Barranger, OP who at that time was the Prior at St. Stephen's Priory in Dover, MA offered to be his Spiritual Advisor and Danny eagerly accepted. Father Barranger's generous offer was fortuitous and, later described by Danny as vital on his path to priesthood.

Subsequently, Father Barranger suggested to Danny that he might like to attend the Easter Vigil at St. Stephen's Priory. I was surprised and pleased when Danny invited me to attend the Vigil with him. Why wouldn't I be pleased to accompany him? The two of us customarily attended the Easter Vigil together. In the confinement of a small Chapel and with a small congregation consisting mostly of Dominicans, the enormity of the Resurrection Of Christ seemed to become a tangible reality. We were profoundly moved. Exsultet!

Effortlessly juggling sports and parties as usual, Danny managed to keep his private pledge to deepen his prayer life. April 2001 brought his first Boston Marathon — the first of nine marathons he would run in six years. To Alice and me, his life still looked like a study of perpetual motion.

Regardless of his top-speed life, he was always available for a friend in need. In a crisis, Danny was the first one called, and after his death we heard countless stories of how he always had the right words of counsel. I was not surprised by those stories, for from his childhood Danny thrived on helping others. Compassion and service were part of his being, and his response was always quick and direct: "What do you need? How can I help?"

His friend, Dr. Joe Ciccone's litany is typical:

"Danny showing up with the rest of the goons at my father's funeral in New Jersey; ... conversations on the beach at 4:00 a.m.; ...when he helped me move from Boston to New Jersey on that hot August day; ... driving the Kennedy family station wagon to get coffee down the Cape; ... his warm eyes and pats on the shoulder..."

Marguerite Cail, a childhood and college friend, said later, "He did make you feel as if you were the only one in the room."

In secular terms Dan manifested a magnetic personality. But his appeal was in a deeper sense a spiritual attractiveness — the fruit of his extraordinary inner joy and his ever-deepening love for the Lord. As Father William B. Palardy, a former member of the faculty at St. John's Seminary and currently the Rector of Saint Pope John XXIII National Seminary said; "Dan reflected a contagious love for Christ." Father Palardy's perceptive observation capsulized Dan's inner zeal for the Lord. He did not 'leave 'his light' under a bushel basket. Dan's light did; shine before others. (Matthew 5:15)

Throughout his twenties, Danny was on a pilgrimage to find God's will, and his pace kept picking up speed. Interviewed a few years later for the archdiocesan newspaper, Danny recalled his career this way:

> "I had a great job, great pay, great travel opportunities…a terrific girlfriend. With all that, the fact that the priesthood was rattling around in my head gave me pause. As I took steps to investigate this notion, God began to make it clearer to me."

One summer's evening in the year 2001, Alice, Danny and I dined at Clancy's Restaurant in Dennisport. As Danny proceeded to enjoy the omnipresent clam chowder he always ordered, much to Alice's chagrin he quickly put a smile on her face when he informed us that he decided to request a one-year Leave of Absence from Cabot Corporation to enter St. John's Seminary in Brighton, MA. Cabot Corporation executives were supportive. They deemed his objective to be admirable and assured him if he desired to return to Cabot Corporation at the expiration of the one-year Leave of Absence there would be position available for him.

Despite years of trying to discern while juggling a busy job, travel, and his social life, Danny still did not know whether he had a vocation to the priesthood. Surely in the seminary he at last would be able to focus on the most important question of his life, which required his full attention. At least he thought so – and we concurred. At long last, acquiescence achieved.

Alice and I were delighted with his decision and were transfixed as he chronicled the years and years of deliberation that brought him to this impactful decision. He felt that follow-up visits to St. John's Seminary after attending the Cardinal's Retreat combined with frequent meetings with Father Barranger clarified the reality of his vocation.

Alice ordered a celebratory second glass of chardonnay and I, a second glass of Glenfiddick. Danny of course, in recognition of his 'Bud Man' days, ordered a second bottle of his trusty Bud Light, the beer he used to distribute for Quality Beverage Corp.

Chapter 7: Embarking on Seminary Life

"Speak, Lord, for your servant is listening." (Samuel 3:9b)

As things turned out, Dan's ability to discern would be the least of the challenges he would confront in his first year at St. John's Seminary in Brighton, MA.

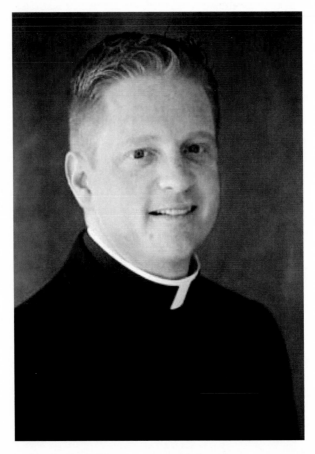

In the Fall of 2001, Danny entered the six-year program, which comprises two years of Pre-Theology and a four-year Theology track, along with summer internships at parishes and Catholic institutions. He was pleased that St. John's Seminary accepted credit for Philosophy and Theology courses he completed at Providence College thus he was allowed to enter as a second Pre-theology seminarian which meant he would be placed in the Ordination Class of 2006. Five years had passed since he graduated college, and potentially five years away from standing at the Altar *in Persona Christi*.

The caliber of men at St. John's Seminary impressed Dan. Many of them had sacrificed significant careers to enter the seminary. He met attorneys, carpenters, stockbrokers, Marines, Air Force pilots, and doctors. Some were gregarious, others shy or cerebral, but all shared a seriousness of purpose in following God's will for their lives. As a rule, any friend of the Church was a friend of Dan's, and his ready smile and open nature found him an easy welcome among upperclassmen and newbies alike.

St. John's Seminary barely commenced its fall semester when on September 11, 2001, a horrible day in the history of the United States occurred. Who can forget the shock, the horror, and the frightening days that followed, with silent skies where no planes flew?

Seminarians were not immune to the roiling emotions that engulfed the nation; fortunately the faculty and spiritual directors guided them well. For weeks seminarians and faculty spoke incessantly in and out of the classrooms about horror of the attack and the effect that it had on Boston as two of the planes that were crashed emanated from Boston. Difficult days, hard lessons: the appalling grief of an unexpected loss, the burden of anger, and the difference between zeal and zealotry. Seminarians quickly learned, suffering conveys powerful lessons of faith, hope, and yes, love — an understanding they would need for their future work as priests.

A second horror arrived literally on their doorstep that winter, when TV satellite trucks and packs of reporters set up camp outside the seminary. January 6, 2002 marked the origin of the Boston Globe's groundbreaking exposé on the decades of clergy abuse of minors and the subsequent cover-up by Church leaders. Barely hiding their disdain, the reporters accosted the seminarians, demanding to know: "How could anyone in his right mind want to become a priest?"

Day after day the investigative series unfolded, fresh allegations emerged, and soon charges were being leveled in dioceses across the country. Like all faithful Catholics, Danny was appalled that officials, relying on questionable psychological and medical advice, opted to protect the institution rather than innocent victims. Believers and nonbelievers alike felt repulsed and betrayed by the scandal.

In retrospect, we learned the extent of the abuse and cover-ups was not as pervasive as the media presumed. The Jay Report found that a small percentage of the ordained clergy committed nearly one-quarter of the offenses, and, in fact, less than 5 percent of active clergy were guilty. Still, just one priest exploiting one child was inexcusable, and throughout Dan's seminary years the brush of scandal and suspicion tarred every member of the clergy. Bill Lohan, a seminarian at the time, recalls Dan's reaction:

"The sex abuse scandal certainly was an overarching shadow over those years. Dan took a militaristic and sports-like stand towards it all. He believed even though we were few, we were the beginning of a new generation that could win

back the trust of the people — not overnight; the seminary told us candidly that we would be digging the church out of this hole for the rest of our lives. Dan knew and accepted that and saw it as an important challenge."

What sort of man would want to become a priest? That spring when the question was lobbed at Dan, he hit it out of the ballpark. Calling in to a Boston Sports Radio Talk Program, Dan eloquently denounced the traitorous defection of Red Sox star pitcher Roger Clemens to the Toronto Blue Jays. The hosts liked his spirited argument and wanted to know more about this caller: "Dan from Needham, what do you do for a living?"

When Dan replied, "I called to speak about Clemens not to discuss my occupation". They persisted and he eventually took the bull by the horns and said; I'm a seminarian at St. John's Seminary in Brighton," the hosts gasped. "What do you really do?" they demanded, incredulously. "Are you crazy? With all that's being said about the priest crisis you expect us to believe that?"

Danny had a simple answer: This was about God and him, nobody else. He explained:

"I was employed by a large international corporation, with a promising future, when I decided to take a leave of absence and enter St. John's Seminary. I was anxious to determine if the Lord wanted me to work for Him."

Danny's unapologetic frankness impressed the hosts. "Good for you, 'Dan from Needham,'" they told him. "That's a wonderful story."

Shortly after the radio conversation Danny was asked to speak on behalf of vocations after weekend Masses at St. Agnes Church in Arlington, MA. The Pastor, Father Brian Flatley, suggested that he greet parishioners after Masses. Naturally he incorporated his brief radio appearance in his vocation talk at St. Agnes. After one of the Masses, to his delight, a nun came up to shake his hand, "I heard you on the radio!" she laughed. "You were wonderful, the best affirmation of vocations that I've heard in years. Thank you, 'Dan from Needham'!"

A bright spot for all the seminarians in Danny's first year was the pride they felt when their Rector, Father Richard Lennon, was ordained an Auxiliary Bishop of Boston. He continued as Rector of St. John's guiding seminarians with a steady hand through the continuing turmoil confronting the Church of Boston until he was appointed Apostolic Administrator upon Cardinal Law's resignation in December 2002.

Brotherhood

May your hand be on the man you have chosen, the man you have given your strength. (Psalm 80:18)

In the fall of 2001, St. John's Seminary opened the seminary doors for Family Day; it was our first visit to St. John's Seminary, As Alice and I were feeling uneasy as we stood in the foyer uncertain as to where we should go. Suddenly, Alice gleefully called out in relief, "Here comes Danny!" I turned and spotted a familiar figure striding rapidly toward us with a huge grin on his face. As he approached the two of us he welcomed Alice with a kiss and a big hug. When he turned to greet me, beaming with an ear-to-ear smile, he unmercifully administered his customary bone-breaking handshake that he loved to inflict upon me. I retaliated with every ounce of strength I could muster. In the crowded foyer of St.

John's Seminary, were utilizing every ounce of our strength to compel the other into submission. No words were ever exchanged during this father-son family ritual until Alice invariably intervened; "Danny stop, you're hurting your father". Thankfully, he always complied with his mother's request. Boy, how I miss those bone crushing handshakes. "Thus says the Lord of hosts: Let your hands be strong..." (Zechariah 8:9)

It was a thrill for both of us to tour St. John's Seminary. The Chapel, the Refectory, and classrooms are contained in the same edifice. Alice and I were in awe of the absolutely beautiful Chapel with images of the twelve apostles adorning the nave. Seminarians were seated in graduated rows facing across the center aisle with the Altar at the far end of the Chapel.

Throughout Family Day, we were introduced to one after another of our son's newest seminary pals, many of whom would soon become frequent visitor to our Needham home.

A frequent visitor at our home was Matt Westcott; a lawyer, ex-Marine, and former stand-up comedian. Matt always kept Alice and I in stiches; he always told hilarious stories. Frequently Danny would call and tell me not to go to bed early because Matt was coming over tonight. When Matt was visiting I could always count on staying up late and laughing until well past my bedtime. Another visitor whom Dan nicknamed "Broadway Bob" was Bob Blaney. For over ten years, Bob had been an actor, singer, and accomplished pianist on Broadway, thus Danny's nomenclature upgrade. The St. John's gang was always welcome at our house.

Fr. Dan's and Fr. Matt Westcott's Ordination Day

Dan Hennessey was a fourth-year theology student preparing for ordination in May 2002 spoke with our son Danny at great length about the importance discernment plays on the path to priesthood. Hennessey would go on to be appointed the Archdiocese of Boston's Vocation Director only a few years after ordination. The elder Dan promised the younger one that after three years at St. John's Seminary he would receive clarity of the Lord's will for him: "Give it a fair chance and you will know." This upperclassman's kindness and thoughtful advice helped Danny to find his footing. Those words of encouragement sustained him during his seminary journey even when certainty always seemed to be on the horizon, never quite within grasp — as frustratingly elusive as a mirage.

Danny had no time for gossip or whining. His default mode was to be upbeat and funny, and his positive personality was contagious and encouraging to others. He was always lightening the mood for other seminarians in the Common Room after a long day of classes and discernment. Father Matt Westcott recalled appreciatively:

"His down-to-earth pragmatism and humor helped many men keep their feet on the ground. When the difficulties of seminary life come along, there can be a tendency to brood. Dan effectively popped those bubbles of gloom."

It helped that many seminarians shared Dan's love of sports. The camaraderie of watching a game together on television or playing a pickup game outdoors blows off steam and helps cement connections.

Seminarian Jeff Statz, who graduated from The Franciscan University in Steubenville, Ohio, reflected the same traditional Catholic values instilled in Dan at Providence College and he was as rabid a sports enthusiast as Dan. The two organized a seminary softball team, which continues to this day. Dan and Jeff's enthusiasm convinced Boston College to admit the St. John's Seminary Softball Team into their intra-mural league. Both of them were often seen slamming the ball over the fence at Shea Field on Boston College Campus where they had enough enjoyment on the field to take the sting out of their frequent defeats.

Seminarian Statz, whose birthday is January 27th, coincidentally, the day Dan died in 2008, selected Danny to proclaim a Reading at his Ordination in Manchester, New Hampshire. At that time, Danny was on a leave of absence from the seminary. Father Statz' gesture was critical for Dan in turning the tide of his discernment toward a return to St. John's.

Father Bill Lohan recalls another extracurricular activity of Danny and Darin Colarusso, a former United States Air Force fighter pilot:

> *"Some of the faculty would try to get some of the softer, introverted guys to hang out with Dan to toughen them up a bit. He and Darin Colarusso (now a priest) were teaching some of the guys how to lift weights."*

Few classmates golfed, but Dan's golf clubs were never far away (i.e. the trunk of his car). Once he learned that seminarians played free at the Putterham Golf Club in Brookline, he was in seventh heaven. Bishop Richard G. Lennon, the Rector, knew of Dan's interest in golf and selected him to serve on a formative committee to inaugurate an annual St. John's Golf Tournament Fundraiser. The first St. John's Seminary Golf Tournament was held in Fall of 2001. It continues today and currently dedicates a portion of its proceeds to the Reverend Daniel J Kennedy Memorial Scholarship.

When a team of seminary evaluators visited St. John's Seminary as part of the U.S. Conference of Catholic Bishops' response to the abuse crisis, upon arrival at Logan Airport an evaluator that Dan was driving back to Brighton spotted golf clubs in the trunk of his car. Anticipating that he might be chided for frivolity, instead, Dan won a commendation. The evaluator, Father Michael C. Barber, SJ considered recreation essential for all clergymen and he pronounced in a general meeting of St. John's Seminarians that golf or tennis are excellent activities for the clergy. Dan was thrilled to learn that his interest in golf had official sanction — although he would have, in all probability, continued to play golf in his spare time.

In late autumn Dan decided to train for his 2nd Boston Marathon. He had continued running long distance for pleasure and to stay fit, but a marathon requires three months or more of extensive training; moreover, to obtain an official number for the Boston Marathon he had to first squeeze in a qualifying marathon elsewhere. Even if he could run a preliminary marathon would his speed be fast enough to qualify? Doubtful. He was an atypical runner, built more like a football player, not the conventional lean, long legged, loping svelte runner.

More importantly, could he maintain his grades and not skimp on St. John's rigorous regimen of daily discernment? Questionable. Consequently, there was no avenue available for him to obtain a 'bib' aka Marathon Number.

Unexpectedly, a sympathetic faculty member, Father Robert Flagg, short-circuiting the formal procedure, procured an official number aka a 'bib'. Dan wore his bib proudly on Marathon Monday (Patriots' Day) in April 2002, determined not to disgrace his supporters — and to his delight he succeeded in finishing the Marathon with a time of 4 hours and 30 minutes; he was only seconds off his previous time running his first marathon in 2001.

Dan's friends had no doubts he would finish the race. As Bob Blaney recalled; "Dan was an intense individual and generally achieved his objective. Whatever goal he set for himself, he sought with full commitment." Bob was correct; Danny never minced words, was direct, and confronted every issue head-on.

Ever gregarious, Danny seemed to know half the people in the world and seemed to maintain contact with all of them, wherever they wandered. He was not reticent about putting his contacts to use. When he found out that the seminarians would have to sleep on a gym floor before the annual Washington, D.C., March for Life on January 22, he immediately reached for the phone. Beds are hard to find when hundreds of thousands pour in from all over the country. A good friend from undergraduate days at Providence College, Brother James "Mike" Cuddy, a seminarian at the Dominican House of Studies in Washington, graciously arranged accommodations for the St. John's crew. Well rested, "Dan the Fixer" marched proudly with his fellow seminarians, prayerful witnesses to the sanctity of life.

The Good Samaritan

And how can people preach unless they are sent? (Romans 10:15a)

Unlike college, there is no summer recess for seminarians. After rigorous fall and spring semesters, seminarians are assigned to various parishes in the Archdiocese. The pastor, as the seminarian's on-site supervisor, provides living accommodations in a guest room. During the internship, the seminarian sees the wide range of responsibilities and duties encountered by parish priests; from the mundane to the tragic. Dan was assigned to St. Edward's Parish in Brockton, MA with the primary to responsibility to serve as Pastoral Minister at Good Samaritan Hospital.

Pastor-supervisors selected by St. John's Seminary to oversee seminarian summer assignments portray a love for the priesthood and a love for parishioners. The Pastor of St. Edward's, Father Jim Flavin, was no exception. Father Flavin understood that many seminarians endure a degree of trepidation in their first field assignment so he made certain that a welcoming atmosphere permeated

St. Edward's. Thankfully, Dan settled in well. Father Jim was intent on making Dan feel comfortable as introduced him to the staff, parishioners, politicians, funeral directors, etc. As Father Flavin intended, Dan's circle of friends seemed to increase exponentially. He was most pleased with his summer assignment in Brockton.

Father Flavin was also sensitive to non-spiritual needs of seminarians. To offset a loss of income, he offered Dan a side job; painting church property. He even allowed Dan's seminarian friend, Matt Westcott who was assigned to another parish, to join Dan on various painting projects. Between Dan and Matt, a former stand-up comedian, the two of them were a reincarnation of the comedian team, Abbott and Costello. Instead of 'Who's on First?' it was 'Who's (First) on the Ladder'?

At Good Samaritan Hospital, Dan began developing the formal pastoral skills essential in caring for sick and dying people under the tutelage of the Hospital Chaplain. One day, he saw a note that no Catholic clergyman was to visit a patient (that we'll call "Jim").

Once Dan determined a course of action he was never known to hesitate, he was full steam ahead with the implementation of his plan. The hospital's prohibition was all the motivation Dan needed. He made a beeline up to Jim's room, knocked on the door, entered the room and introduced himself as a representative of the Chaplain's Office.

Jim was steaming mad; he was furious and he immediately began to berate the church and he does not want to see any priest! With venom in his voice and ferocity in his eyes he glared menacingly at the unwelcome guest. When Jim drew a breath Dan interrupted and calmly said, "I'm not a priest. I'm just a seminarian."

Silence. "A seminarian?" Jim asked. "I used to be a seminarian."

On this common ground the two began to talk. After a few minutes Jim agreed to allow a priest to visit him. Initially, the Chaplain was dismayed that Dan deliberately disobeyed instructions and visited Jim. His distaste for Dan's disobedience quickly abated when he learned that Jim now was receptive to a visit by a priest. The enthusiastic Chaplain rushed up to 'forbidden hospital room' — only to be repelled, badgered and berated. Within minutes an agitated Chaplain returned. Now steam was billowing from the Chaplain-supervisor and vituperation emitting from his frothing mouth! The irate Chaplain thought; did Dan purposely set him up for humiliation?

When the steam from the Chaplain's ire began to abate Dan prevailed upon him to accompany him back to Jim's room. With his typical tenacity of purpose Dan bounded back up the stairs to Jim's room with the Chaplain-Supervisor trailing behind. Whereupon he suggested that the Chaplain remain in the hallway while he, alone, re-entered the lion's den. Sternly, with an intense expression and penetrating eyes Dan confronted Jim and said; "Jim did you or did you not give me *your word* that you would be receptive to a visit from a priest?" "Yes," Jim sheepishly admitted, but he had changed his mind. Like a coach reprimanding his best player, Dan addressed Jim man to man. "As a former seminarian, Jim, you know when you give your word you cannot renege on your *commitment*," he chided. "Now I'm going to bring in the priest, and you are going to keep *your word*." Jim did not dissent. Dan left; the Chaplain came in and a lengthy conversation ensued between Jim and the Chaplain.

Later, the Chaplain thanked Dan both for taking the initiative to tackle this challenge and for seeing it through to fruition. This incident typifies his intensity and determination augmented with a direct approach; he did not, 'beat around the bush'. As Father Bob Blaney said, "Father Dan was bold — and never afraid to be real." In his brother Jack's words, "He took serious matters seriously and lighter matters with ease and humor and he was gifted in assimilating the serious with the lighter." It was a powerful blend.

Another assignment for Dan during the summer and fall of 2002 was to be a Pastoral Minister at the Jeanne Jugan Residence in Somerville. The Jeanne Jugan Residence is a highly acclaimed home for the elderly administered by the Little Sisters of the Poor. Since boyhood, Dan spent many hours visiting elderly neighbors; he did not need to be told that the elderly, however frail, have dignity and deserve respect. He absolutely loved the elderly. While the Sisters' loving care of the residents impressed him deeply,

Dan's cheerful attentiveness and eagerness to serve the residents impressed the nuns. After his ordination in 2008, they invited Father Dan back to celebrate Mass for the residents.

Seminary Life, Year Two

Be still and know I am God. (Psalm 46:10)

Dan knew his decision to join the seminary made my mother, Eileen Kennedy, happy. Danny and Gram grew closer as she aged, and in her last years he often phoned just to 'talk' and, on occasion, unbeknown to anyone, he drove the 90 miles to Chicopee for a visit with his grandmother.

Dan never mentioned these conversations and visits to us as he treasured his personal life. Dan and Gram were very different. Dan was outgoing, Gram was reserved; Dan was gregarious and spoke his mind authoritatively, and Gram guarded her words. Somehow they found common ground, and when he told Gram he was entering St. John's Seminary she proudly announced, "I am going to have a party for Danny, because I won't be around when he becomes a priest." Reserved, stoic Gram throwing a party? Her exuberance was obvious and, she fulfilled her promise and, thanks to Gram, we had a wonderful family reunion in celebration of Danny's "new job."

It wasn't long until Dan reached the point in his seminary tenure when he was authorized to wear the Roman Collar; Gram came through again and she financed the purchase of his black suit and, Roman Collar. The first time he wore the clerics Gram purchased was September 15, 2002, when he visited Gram in the Mercy Medical Center in Springfield, the day before she died.

Danny served as an acolyte at Gram's Funeral Mass and wore the alb my sister, Aunt Judy gave him. For several years Judy was Gram's sole caregiver for years and she was grateful for the love and thoughtfulness Danny continually communicated to Gram.

As Dan was wrapping up his fall classes, he was interviewed by Catholic Memorial High School's magazine for the spring 2003 issue; "Alumni Profile." The idea of a vocation had first occurred to him seriously in college, Dan said, but he had no regrets about his years of corporate globetrotting:

"Five years of living life, paying bills, and having fun was the best asset I could have brought into the seminary. It gives me a broader perspective on things. What I have learned is that if you do have a vocation to the priesthood, you'd be unhappy anywhere else."

The interviewer pressed the point: had the former Silver Knight been called to priesthood? Dan refused to be pinned down, however. "I'm actively pursuing whatever it is that the Lord wants me to do," he answered. "St. John's Seminary is assisting me in determining the proper path for me." Whether God wanted him to live a religious or lay vocation mattered less to Dan than being certain of God's plan, and he was willing to let certitude play itself out.

Perturbed by St. John's Seminary's declining enrollment, Dan was eager to spread the word to more men that God was still calling, if only they would listen. It is hard enough for faithful Catholic men to consider vocations but the shadow of the abuse scandal made it more difficult. He yearned to see the St. John's Seminary Chapel once again filled to capacity.

Dan told me that at one point a seminarian confided to him that others had been taunting him for one reason or another. Dan loved to tease — and be teased — however, it was clear to him that this man's plight was no joke. Seminary life often presents challenges a man has to overcome, but obviously cruelty has no place there, so Dan demanded names, resolving to go to each one and address his behavior directly. Sometimes a hockey player has to take an adversary or malcontent to the boards, and Dan always subscribed to immediate action. Procrastination or hesitancy was never in his vocabulary!

Spiritual formation requires a strong prayer life; seminarians spend a considerable amount of time in community prayer and in private prayer. In addition to daily Mass and reading the Liturgy of the Hours, weekdays include a Holy Hour consisting of Eucharistic Exposition, Silent Meditation, Vespers, and Benediction. As the student handbook explains:

"This daily time with Jesus in the Blessed Sacrament fosters a seminarian's intimacy with Christ, and also gives him the absolutely necessary time for silence, without which he cannot hope to hear the Lord speaking to him."

All seminarians meet frequently with Spiritual Directors. Dan was blessed to have been assigned to an outstanding spiritual director who was indispensible in his discernment process. He considered his spiritual director to have been a gift from God. He told Alice and me that a spiritual director is not to be akin to the buddy-buddy concept or a big brother as in college but a man who is able to assist the seminarian in his spiritual development. Seminarians also practice Lectio Divina, meditative prayer on passages of Scripture, to identify application of the Word of God to their individual lives. This practice of internalizing Scripture is a great aid as they advance to the point of preparing homilies and counseling individuals.

Few of these forms of prayer were new to Dan. He had been exposed to Benediction and Exposition of the Eucharist on First Fridays as a child and as an Altar Server. He also enhanced his love for Eucharistic Adoration while attending Providence College. In fact, long before coming to St. John's Seminary Dan discovered the paradox of Eucharistic Adoration: the more time he spent with Jesus in the Eucharist, the easier his life went when away from Him, for he held Jesus more closely in his mind and heart as he went about his day.

Name the Real Seminarian

How beautiful are the feet of those who bring the good news! (Romans 10:15b)

One sign of Dan's spiritual growth at St. John's Seminary was the confidence with which he exhibited in daily conversation. He always expressed his ideas with confidence but now we detected a deeper and more profound tone to his conversations. His demeanor seemed to reflect an inner joy, a spiritual joy, which became more and more obvious as he progressed in the seminary. Not everyone is sufficiently skilled in the use of wit to develop a serious point, but Dan had that knack and he adroitly utilized it when conversing with people especially skeptics. It was of course a gift from God, an endearing quality which was enhanced by the solid educational and spiritual environment of St. John's Seminary.

Since his first day as a seminarian, Dan volunteered to speak any time a notice was posted seeking a seminarian to offer a vocations talk at a parish or a CCD or Confirmation Class. As Matt Westcott recalled:

"Eager to be active in vocations, Dan would take it on himself to volunteer for virtually all of the Vocations Office events when a seminarian was requested. He saw this as his way not only of encouraging vocations but as making sure the best guys and best kinds of guys were being encouraged. He would often recruit me to join him. His eagerness and willingness to get out into the crowds of teens or other young men was always impressive. I think his background in the corporate world helped him a lot in this."

The audience, whoever that may have been, probably expected a dry lecture, but Dan preferred to be creative and he devised skits and/or games to capture their attention. He loved using humor to break down barriers and to heal hearts.

One skit, "Name the Real Seminarian," placed Dan alongside two secular friends, all three dressed casually. Each spoke briefly, then the students proceeded to determine which of them was studying to become a priest. Dan committed to dispel the perception that possessing a strong spiritual life and having fun are mutually exclusive. Of course, Dan was covertly teaching his pals the same lesson as the students, for he had their spiritual growth in mind as well.

Dan was delighted when St. John's Seminary Administrators entrusted him with the responsibility to be Master of Ceremonies (MC) for all seminary liturgical functions. The position required a familiarization with rubrics and a multitude of liturgical procedures. Dan was, by nature methodically oriented so it wasn't long before he utilized his work-world experience and computerized instruction manuals, training programs, and systematized schedules replete with responsibility reminders. This proved to be a forerunner for the Altar Server programs he would implement on his parish assignments. He believed that proper training programs would in-still confidence and thus provide joy for the seminarians assigned to liturgical services. The training program incorporated formal instruction in aspects of speech, demeanor, and liturgical norms. During his tenure with the seminary's liturgy professor, with Father Christopher J. Coyne, who is now the Bishop of the Diocese of Burlington in Vermont. They shared a love of liturgy as well as New England Patriots football!

The MC position was in some sense a sacrifice for Dan, who loved to slip into the chapel and lose himself in private prayer. Those days were somewhat curtailed when chapel time became a responsibility albeit a joyful responsibility In the course of his daily duties Dan was able to inculcate time in his schedule to allot time to visit with Jesus in the Tabernacle with his ever-present breviary at his side.

Matt Westcott, Dan's assistant MC, understood Dan's mixed feelings, but saw the task as good training for priesthood:

"This was a topic we talked about since attending a prayer-ful liturgy and celebrating (or even emceeing) a prayerful liturgy are two very different things and there is a steep learning curve necessary for the new priest. Seminarians are blessed to go to Mass at the seminary, where the prop-er, dignified, and beautiful celebration of all the Church's rites are demanded. This isn't an obsession with rubrics. It's so that the man, once he leaves the seminary and goes to the parish, has the correct model of liturgy to implement in his parish."

"But the correct theology and liturgical model is the easy part. How does the new priest pray at Mass when he also

has to be in charge and keep an eye on the smooth func-
tioning of the Mass? The answer is — there is no answer.
The new priest simply must get used to it as something
asked of him as a priest."

With all his Vocations talks, Dan's effectiveness as a motivational speaker spread. When the president of Boston College, Father William P. Leahy, SJ, established a Vocation Committee, he asked Father John A. Farren, OP, the rector of St. John's, to appoint a seminarian as a representative and Dan was chosen. His contributions so impressed Father Leahy that he invited Dan to meet with a collegiate committee to discuss a program to promote vocations at Boston College. (His Jesuit Hockey coach, Papa Leo, would have been pleased!)

Though the committee met frequently, it was relatively easy for Dan to participate because Boston College's main campus is directly across Commonwealth Avenue in Brighton. That proximity also made it easy for Dan to attend Boston College Varsity Hockey games, and he was even invited to skate in the early morning priests' hockey program. Dan lived the maxim that a true hockey player always keeps his skates at hand.

Likewise, a true runner never turns down a race. When Father Dan Hennessey became the Director of Vocations for the Archdiocese, he suggested that Dan run the Marathon in an effort to promote vocations to the priesthood. Dan was delighted to accept both a black tee-shirt reading Vocations to the Priesthood and that precious item, a bib number.

From the Starting Line in Hopkinton, MA to the Finish Line in Back Bay in Boston, on the entire 26.2-mile route, Dan proudly displayed both the shirt and the bib. His goal was twofold that year; his omni-present determination to finish the race was in unison with another goal, Promoting Vocations.

Danny stopping to hydrate near St. John's Seminary
during the 2006 Boston Marathon.

He explained his "Theology of Running" to a Pilot Newspaper reporter. "Running is similar to discerning a vocation," Dan said. "There is quiet time which allows a runner to pray and to contemplate the will of God." He was describing his ordinary runs, of course, not the grueling ordeal of a marathon; on his everyday runs when he regularly prayed the Rosary. "He worked hard to keep himself physically fit, academically sharp, and, most importantly, he prayed to remain *spiritually strong*." said Father Jim DiPerri.

Summer in the United States Navy

Meanwhile the boat, already a few miles offshore, was being tossed about
by the waves, for the wind was against it.
(Matthew 14:24)

Dan's summer assignment in 2003 was unique; he applied for and was accepted into, Naval Chaplains School at the Naval Station in Newport, Rhode Island. A good friend from high school days, Michael Becker, a graduate of the United States Naval Academy and a Lieutenant in the United States Navy just completed his training at the Naval Special Warfare Training Center in California and was commissioned a United States Navy SEAL. Dan admired Mike's accomplishment — as well as his dashing white uniform. Although this was not the typical seminarian summer assignment, Dan was determined to explore military service. Father (later Cardinal) John O'Connor from Philadelphia, PA was a Navy Chaplain, why not 'Dan from Needham'?

When Dan returned to Needham after a summer in Navy Boot Camp he proudly displayed his Navy uniform and, his military haircut; *red hair, gone*! His head was shaved to the scalp! What have they done to my son? This reminds me of what Danny said to Alice when he was four or five years old as his sisters perpetually teased him about having red hair. He said when he died he was going to ask 'God-ie' to give him brown hair! (Hopefully he had more substantive topics to discuss).

One day while he was home, Dan and I ran into an old friend who hardly recognized him. With a serious expression, I explained that, both of us were in disguise. We were concealing our red hair; Dan shaved his off, and I dyed mine, gray. That earned me smiles from both of them. I do think Dan 'disguised' his jealousy; for once I had beaten him to a punch line.

Chapter 8: Scituate Harbor

I am your servant; give me discernment that I may know your testimonies.
(Psalm 119:125)

In 2004, Dan was assigned to St. Mary of the Nativity Parish in Scituate Harbor which is a beautiful community south of Boston, in the area generally referred to as 'the South Shore'. The name 'Scituate' is from an Indian Tribe meaning 'cold brook'. The 'cold brook' flows to the inner harbor and it is a wonderful aquatic environment. Scituate is also one of the few locations on the Atlantic coast where Irish Moss grows. The emerald green plant tolerates moist climates and Scituate Harbor is certainly moist. This may explain why the Town of Scituate annually features a highly acclaimed St. Patrick's Day Parade.

Dan's Intern Supervisor was the Pastor of St. Mary of the Nativity, Father Brian Manning. Father Manning was experienced in tutoring seminarians. The predecessor seminarian intern who Father Manning mentored at St. Mary of the Nativity was Father Michael Drea who was ordained to the presbyterate in May 2004.

After arriving in Scituate one of the first things Dan did was look for a road along the ocean where he could continue his marathon training. When he asked Father Manning if he could recommend a 'route to run on,' the pastor responded that he could provide a path; a 'Path to Priesthood'. Deo Gracias.

Father Manning was a major blessing for Dan; they really synced. Both of them had much in common; they were bright, possessed an intense love for Jesus Christ and were 'quick-witted'.

Dan was grateful that Father Manning involved him in so many of the parish ministries at St. Mary's which enabled him to obtain firsthand experience in the day-to-day function of a parish. Father Manning observed, "Dan possessed inner strength and determination. Certainly his faith in the Lord Jesus was the great motivator of his 'race' to serve the Lord and to finish the Marathon." He added, "Dan took seriously the demands of preparation and he trained hard to be a priest. Dan knew and lived the Mercy and Goodness of God. It was not always easy for him but he kept his eyes and heart on God as he persevered."

Friends beget friends

Where there is doubt, faith…Where there is darkness, light..
(St. Francis of Assisi)

Dan's painting career and, the remuneration it generated during his summer at St. Edward in Brockton, dissipated when he relocated to Scituate. St. Mary's of the Nativity was recently painted so he needed to improvise. He did discover other opportunities to obtain income just as he did during his boyhood years on Cape Cod. An occasional substitute teaching assignment at Catholic Memorial High School was helpful in a financial sense but it was a joy for him to be educating young students. Renewing his AHAUS Referee Certification was also helpful, plus it kept him involved with one of his favorite sports, hockey.

More lucrative and also enjoyable, though limited to semester breaks and occasional weekends — and not mentioned loudly at the seminary — was his job as night bouncer at the Corrib Pub and Grill in West Roxbury. It was a great match for a well-muscled guy with a sharp eye for troublemakers and a smooth tongue to defuse confrontations.

The Corrib was popular with Dan's old high school pals — Catholic Memorial was not far away — and soon he began to acquire a new circle of West Roxbury friends. The proprietor of 'The Corrib', the Bligh family, knew Dan from his CM days plus they liked having a seminarian on the staff. It wasn't long before his pal Matt Westcott was also on the payroll. Three cheers to the Bligh family for offering 'after hour training' for seminarians.

Dan was always convivial, anxious to exchange ideas with anyone and everyone he had a gift for listening which generated a comfortable forum so others would feel free to share their hopes and fears with him. Father Chip Hines, who was an upperclassman when Dan entered St. John's Seminary recalls, "My most prevalent memory of him is his 'humanity,' his ability to speak to anyone, because he was a regular guy with an extraordinary calling."

Shortly after Dan commenced moonlighting at The Corrib he encountered a patron, Larry McCarthy, who informed Dan that he was a 'fallen-away Catholic'. Immediately, Dan was determined to establish a rapport with Larry. He succeeded and it wasn't long before Larry committed on returning to the sacraments – with a proviso. Larry would go to confession and return to Mass when Danny was ordained to the Holy Priesthood. They shook hands on their 'deal'.

Unfortunately, several months before Dan's ordination, Larry died. Dan was deeply distressed and lamented that he had not insisted on more immediacy in discussing the terms of their agreement.

It was at The Corrib where Dan met another Providence College grad who occasionally passed his time as a part time DJ, in whom he sensed a vocation. Bill Lohan recalls:

"Dan and Matt Westcott were at the pub that night and somehow spoke to one of my friends who directed them to me. I talked for an hour with them. They were normal, well adjusted, and seemed to have similar interests to me. I could see myself being like them and it made the seminarian thing not seem so odd. They were the best advertisement for the priesthood I could have imagined. We became friends instantly."

It wasn't long before Dan brought Bill Lohan an application to the annual 'Cardinal's Discernment Retreat', ultimately culminating with Bill entering St. John's Seminary. Bill and Dan became great friends and it wasn't long before Bill was accompanying Matt on visits to our home in Needham. Father Bill, now a priest in the Archdiocese of Boston, recalls his time as the Corrib's Part time DJ:

"There were nights we were both working there, a seminarian at the door and another playing the music. People who knew us thought it was hysterical; people who did not know us didn't believe that we really were seminarians."

It was like another round of "Name the Real Seminarian."

Another newfound friend West Roxbury friend was Richie Gormley, a Funeral Director, commonly recognized as the 'Lord Mayor of West Roxbury' who possessed an engaging personality whose strong faith impressed Dan. Richie and Dan became good friends and it wasn't long before Richie introduced him to a multitude of West Roxbury stalwarts. Among those newbies was Jim

Sweeney and Peter Meagher both of whom were chartered members of the West Roxbury Running Club. Dan joined the West Roxbury Running Club; at long last Dan would be able to structure his Marathon Training Program with the camaraderie of other runners. Richie, Jim, and Peter rolled their eyes as they contemplated this sturdily built, atypical looking runner, who, as a seminarian, was accustomed to kneeling and praying all day enduring a 26.2 mile run.

"Dan encouraged authenticity and always resisted pretense," Father Bob Blaney recalled. One night at The Corrib, Dan had an extensive conversation with a patron who abruptly declared; he was an atheist. With a castigating look in his eyes Dan leaned forward, placed his nose within inches of the patron and said, emphatically, "That's bullshit. You are not an atheist!"

As was his custom, Dan listened well, catalogued the information in his mind and proceeded to offer an intelligent retort. Dan's Catholic heritage came to mind. Utilizing stories from his own background, Dan presumed that the protagonist might come from similar faith filled parents, so he went on the offense (not surprising). He cited the faith of the man's parents, grandparents as well as the witness of aunts and uncles. Dan then walked him through the Proofs of the Existence of God — the abridged bar room version. It was Dan's patented one-two combination punch: first grab their attention, and then bring on the catechesis. Dan had no idea if he made his point as the agitated patron stormed out of The Corrib.

There are numerous ways to describe Dan's demeanor; direct, no-frills, and to the point. He spoke *boldly; boldly in an enduring way*, not boldly in an offensive way. Although he often spoke in a militant manner, he always spoke with love in his heart.

A week passed with no sign of the man, then one night he returned and greeted Dan contritely; "Dan, I've been thinking about our conversation and I have two things to say." "First, you are right: I am not an atheist." Second, "I have contacted a priest and want to be received back into the Catholic Church". Like St. Paul, who spoke whatever language his listeners required, Dan could pitch his enthusiasm for the Word of God to any audience, even in applying local intonations. Dan also had a faculty to interact with people in their own world, their own area, their own domain, or, on their own turf thus he confiscated fertile terrain in which to cultivate.

Father Matt Westcott observed Dan's unique technique first-hand first while in the seminary and then after ordination:

"Whether sports chat or other casual conversation, Dan had the ability to put others at ease and lead a conversation. This was crucial in getting men to not only discuss vocations and the priesthood but where they were themselves in considering it. Some priests find it a difficult topic to discuss. Not Dan. I have made his 'go for it' style my own in discussing vocations."

A Place Set Apart

I call with all my heart, O Lord; answer me…
(Psalm 119:145)

To recognize Saint John Paul II's twenty-fifth year as pontiff the Knights of Columbus (KofC) reprinted *Gift and Mystery*, his 1996 book written to celebrate fifty years as a priest, and presented a copy to every seminarian in the country. The Supreme Knight, Carl A. Anderson, commenced his cross-country book distribution tour at St. John's Seminary in September 2003. The publicity photo depicts the Supreme Knight with the Rector of St. John's Seminary,

Father John Farren, OP and, Dan Kennedy representing all seminarians at St. John's Seminary.

As a freshman at Providence College, Danny joined the Knights of Columbus (KofC). The Knights reflected the Catholic Church commitment for service to others, were strong defenders of the sanctity of life and unrelenting advocates for vocations to religious life. Immediately he became an active member of Knights working on various projects. The Knights of Columbus have an international reputation espousing their principles of "Faith, Charity, Unity, and Fraternity" and Dan was in the forefront of Providence College Council #5787.

When Dan completed his undergraduate studies he transferred his membership to Needham Council #1611, which held an annual Super Bowl Party to raise funds for archdiocesan seminarians. Dan always enjoyed this event particularly vying with the District Deputy of the Massachusetts Knights of Columbus for the most raffle prizes. Years ago, as a young boy, he learned to squirrel away extra cash for a particular occasion. The K of C Super Bowl Party also provided him with the opportunity to speak with young men and about a priestly vocation. Even in the midst of the football frenzy, Danny's sincere interest always won him a hearing. Privately, he joked that he was planting seeds in fertile ground watered by spilled beer. In 2009, the Supreme Council in New Haven, CT approved renaming the council to: *Father Daniel J. Kennedy Needham Knights of Columbus Council #1611.*

Fr. John Farren, OF, Supreme Knight Carl Anderson and Seminarian Dan.

The Knights also promote vocations, and reprinting and distributing John Paul II's *Gift and Mystery* was one such outreach. The book, a reflection on priesthood, was perfect for seminarians. In their lifetime, they had seen this holy athlete become aged and frail, bent and nearly silenced by Parkinson's disease. He had given all he had to the Church he loved. The example and wisdom of Saint John Paul II were a positive influence at St. John's Seminary throughout the autumn of 2003 that continued beyond his death on April 2, 2005.

Gift and Mystery recalled this saint's childhood, education, life under the Nazi regime, the trials he faced in pursuing his vocation, and the joy he experienced as a pastor. The pope laid out the elements of spiritual development that each seminarian must master, and his book concludes with an inspiring and cautionary challenge: "Learn to see in your priesthood the Gospel treasure for which it is worth giving up everything."

"Giving up everything." Must a man sacrifice all he has for priesthood? These are hard words for seminarians — perhaps meant to give them pause.

Gift and Mystery "was read and treasured by us all," Father Bill Lohan recalls. One reason John Paul's experiences resonated was the turmoil roiling the American Church, and Boston in particular:

> *"The fact that he was in an underground seminary put the scandal that swirled around us in the 2002–2007 years in perspective. Remember that the 2002 sexual scandal was also followed up by the 2004 mass closing of parishes that also scandalized the people and caused deep wounds between neighboring parishes and neighboring priests. We were all happy to be in the seminary and not in the parishes fighting the battle to survive."*

Boston Seminarians also received another dose of papal insight that fall by way of George Weigel, a biographer of John Paul II who also writes about the intersection of Catholic teaching and public policy. Weigel visited the seminary for two days in November 2003, attending Eucharistic Adoration as well as morning and evening prayer. His visit ended with a public address explaining the impact of John Paul II on the Church, from the Theology of the Body and the new Catechism to his insistence that the vocation every Catholic has is to evangelize.

Before delivering his talk, George Weigel paused to comment on what he had observed during his stay:

> *"For all of you who care about the future of the priesthood in the United States and the future of priests in formation here in the Archdiocese of Boston, let me say you have a*

great, great deal to be encouraged by through what is going on here at St. John's Seminary."

His audience, which included Boston's new Archbishop, Seán O'Malley, OFM, was delighted by his praise.

Tougher Classes, Fewer Classmates

The harvest is abundant but the laborers are few. (Matthew 9:37b)

The seminary courses were intensive and they laid a foundation of rigorous analytical skills through the study of Christology, Ecclesiology, Pastoral Counseling, Fundamental Theology, and Moral Theology. Every paper the seminarians wrote and every verbal exchange honed their skills in communicating Christ's love, which would eventually assist them in mastering the art of homiletics — the crucial craft of preaching.

Dan had always been a good student, and although the seminary curriculum was challenging, he absorbed it all and asked for more. His close friend Father Bill Lohan recalled:

"Dan was a bright man who came to the classroom with a critical mind and always worked hard not just to know what the Church teaches, but also why. He didn't just want to know and understand theology, he wanted to be able to teach it and preach in a way that the common man and woman would understand."

Dan insisted there was no excuse for bad preaching and poor catechesis and that all Catholics deserve clear instruction in the faith. Father Bill respected Dan's ability to convey abstract ideas in an understandable, down to earth, vernacular.

"I remember him working on a paper on birth control; he was so excited about teaching people about what the church truly teaches and why. He was firmly convinced that if it were to be explained well, people would understand and accept it even though it seems hard. He really had zeal for desiring to teach, but never in a condescending way. With him it was always trying to put things into practical terms."

Dan's frank, direct, to the point and open nature, combined with his considerable self-confidence, enabled him to freely speak his mind in the classroom or in the common room. After all, he had been an accomplished public speaker since high school, and delivering vocations talks in many venues had burnished his delivery. All these skills transferred well to homiletics.

If anyone asked for assistance with an oral presentation, Dan was happy to help, aware that not everyone is comfortable with public speaking. Sometimes he did not even wait to be asked. When a shy seminarian repeatedly drew sharp criticism from their professor, Danny sought him out to encourage and coach him. Such compassion — as well as his expertise in coolly appraising the strengths and weaknesses of teammates and opponents — would become valuable assets when it came time to study and practice pastoral counseling.

Not only were applications down, but also men were leaving. On the other hand, Dan "often talked about having the integrity to leave as something he respected in others," Matt Westcott recalled. "Many good priests have taken time away from the seminary to discern away from it. Dan respected that." In spite of discouraging moments, seminarians had great hope that Archbishop Sean O'Malley would somehow 'right the ship' and that the future would bring better days.

Better days were ahead, albeit years down the road!

In the words of a 2008 *Boston Globe* article, "a stunning turnabout" seemed to be occurring. The reporter continued:

> "Cardinal Seán P. O'Malley, who resisted calls from priests to close the Catholic seminary when he arrived as Archbishop of Boston five years ago, has made preserving St. John's Seminarian a priority. He has convinced bishops from New England and beyond that the quality of faculty members and the curriculum are outstanding and it is a fertile ground to prepare men for the priesthood. This fall there are 87 men studying theology at St. John's Seminary, an increase from 42 just two years ago."

Pondering and More, Pondering

Anxious, they surge like the sea that cannot calm down.
(Jeremiah 49: 23b)

Dan spent the summer of 2004 at the seaside, but not in the carefree clamming and kite-flying seaside of his youth on Cape Cod with Alice. Between his St. John's Seminary assignment at St. Mary of the Nativity parish in Scituate, and the Newport Naval Base in Newport, RI he was, in a different connotation; *'sea' side for the summer'*.

The months at St. Mary's of the Nativity were busy but more importantly they were happy days. Dan's energy and talent in connecting with parishioners of all ages pleased Father Brian Manning, who was also relieved to find that his intern's organizational skills let him successfully balance his responsibilities in Scituate and Newport. Father Manning became a strong advocate of Dan's priestly vocation, both as a mentor and friend.

The number of boys and girls began to register for Altar Server training increased dramatically that autumn. Father Manning attributed the increased interest to Dan's enthusiastic championing of service to the Church. Likewise, students preparing for Confirmation inquired about becoming Lectors or Extraordinary Ministers. Dan's deep faith and his ever-present joy for life were evident to young and old alike at St. Mary of the Nativity. Everyone made him feel right at home. He was truly 'right at home' when he was with faith-filled people and the parishioners at St. Mary's of the Nativity were definitely, faith-filled people.

Dan enjoyed his wonderful summer-by-the-sea in Scituate and Newport, however, he was deep in thought as clarity of God's will for him remained elusive. His struggle to find certitude continued.

In retrospect, Father Manning compared Dan's discernment challenge to running a marathon:

"Certainly the warmth, goodness and devilish humor of Dan brought many people to the sidelines to help and cheer him on. Dan also took seriously the demands of preparation; he trained hard to be a priest and Dan knew and lived the Mercy and Goodness of God. It was not always easy for him, but Dan kept his eyes and heart on God and persevered."

This discernment dilemma was nothing new; he wrestled with the thought of a vocation for years and was still wrestling. He went on intermittent retreats and spent hours in silent prayer in Eucharistic Adoration chapels but doubts continued to linger. He realized after three years at St. John's Seminary that he possessed the knowledge and people skills required of a priest. What precisely did God want? How could he best serve God with his life? Indecision was foreign to him. He was always able to quickly assess a situation and immediately swing into action; this was different.

Unbeknown to Alice and me, Jack sensed that Dan was not his customary ebullient self so on a hot summer day he invited him to drive down to Simsbury, CT to play some golf and have a few beers. "While my brother was considering whether or not he should take a break from the seminary, he would often escape to Connecticut for a night, weekend, or even afternoon to reflect from a safe distance," Jack recalled.

Dan was first and foremost, a private person; it's doubtful that he shared his discernment dilemma with anyone except his Spiritual Advisor; apparently his brother deciphered the problem. In a sense, as a father, it is gratifying for me to see evidence of brotherly love.

Summer ended and Danny resumed the seminary routine, simultaneously introspective about his future and elated about the immediate present, for his beloved Red Sox were going to the World Series. In October they won — for the first time since 1918 — and even seminarians who professed indifference to sports knew about it, as pandemonium erupted in the hallways and the bells of St. John's began to peal. The culprit who rang the bells without permission was never apprehended, but the fact that the liturgical Master of Ceremonies had knowhow and access — and was a die-hard Red Sox fan — looked highly suspicious.

Tactical Withdrawal

You have need of endurance so that when you have done the will of God you may receive what is promised.
(Hebrews 10:36)

After an enjoyable summer Dan returned to St. John's Seminary in September 2004 slightly sunburned, and purportedly renewed.

As a third-year theology student, he was closing in on the two final years of Advanced Theology, which culminate in ordination first to the Permanent Diaconate and then to the Holy Priesthood of Christ.

In the Fall, Dan continued to alternate between St. John's Seminary in Brighton during the week and St. Mary's of the Nativity in Scituate on weekends. He loved the people at St. Mary's and he loved running the coastline route. Yes, it seemed to be the best of both worlds. He could reflect Christ's Goodness for His people and also could stretch his muscles, replete with sweat and muscular tightness as he ran and ran and ran all the while breathing in deep the aroma of salt air; so invigorating. Dan was intent on running in the Philadelphia Marathon, in November, his fifth marathon.

Dan's obvious joy during in his first three years at St. John's Seminary convinced Alice that he made the right choice when he entered the seminary. While she did sense an aura of reservation as he commenced his fourth year, she attributed it to an excessive workload. When she sensed a semblance of discomfort in Dan — his emotional and spiritual unease — instantaneously she concluded that it was best for him to step back and reassess the direction he was charting for his life.

He was healthy; his Navy Training was rewarding and he was on track for a promotion; the parishioners at St Mary's of the Nativity he served loved him — so what made Dan feel inwardly unsettled?

Jack thought his brother's dilemma stemmed from his absolute determination to have unequivocal certitude. "His discernment was impacted, to a degree, by the clergy misconduct scandal epic center in Boston. That was part of it," Jack said, but the greater issue was that he was emotionally depleted by the inordinate delay in attaining certitude:

"He was always evaluating which path to choose. He was an 'all-in' kind of guy, and once he realized he wasn't 'all in'

anymore, he made the difficult decision to take a break for further reflection."

Father Matt Westcott saw Dan's acceleration from his entry year Class of 2007 to the Class of 2006 as a trigger in that he felt 'rushed' toward the goal and he needed the customary six years to discern. The first two years, Pre-Theology and the following four years, Theology, comprise the six-year program at St. John's Seminary. The final two years of the Theology curriculum are aimed toward the Transitional Diaconate Ordination, and Priesthood Ordination. "I think Dan felt that he was on a conveyor belt toward ordination with men more certain than he was," Father Matt said.

Even though Diaconate Ordination was more than a year away, Dan's doubts became more acute as he contemplated the profundity of the looming commitment. Father Matt points out that, "once you are ordained a deacon, the path is set. You are going to be ordained a priest. You have promised as much to the Church and the Church has promised as much to you. It is the point of no return."

Dan met with the Rector, Father John A. Farren, OP, in January 2005, to request a leave of absence from St. John's Seminary. He informed Father Farren that he had prayed extensively and, over a period of time, discussed this uncertainty with his Spiritual Director. Dan also mentioned that, to his knowledge, none of his seminarian friends had similar misgivings which made him feel 'out of step' in the discernment process.

Father Farren was genuinely surprised. Dan's reports from the faculty and his summer supervisors had always been positive; he was in good standing academically; he enthusiastically participated in all seminary programs — and at age thirty he was hardly an irresolute, changeable youth. Father Farren understood that the prospect of a Diaconate Ordination in 2006 could appear overwhelming if the candidate felt rushed. On the other hand, Dan's apprehension did not change Father Farren's opinion that Dan did in fact have a vocation. Ultimately he concurred with Dan's request to continue to pursue discernment on his own schedule away from St. John's Seminary— and the rector promised a warm welcome should he decide to return.

Dan was most grateful for Father Farren's support, especially his offer of a warm welcome when he returned. He had been concerned that a leave of absence might preclude reapplying to St. John's Seminary. Dan thought back to a conversation he had with Franciscan priest friend, Father Fergus Healey, on a golf course in Halifax, MA.

Father Fergus told him that after being in the seminary for a several years he perceived God's will for him to become cloudy and he became uncertain of his vocation. It was troubling for him in that none of his seminarian brothers had similar trepidations. Father Fergus added that, in those days, if someone left the seminary they would not have an opportunity to return so he stayed and he prayed. Ultimately his uncertainty abated and he was ordained enjoyed many joy filled years as a Franciscan priest.

Dan did not simply vanish from St. John's Seminary. He took time to explain to his seminarian friends that he made an extremely difficult decision to take a leave of absence. The forthcoming diaconate ordination compelled him to confront his reservations. He needed to clear his head in private prayer in a different forum where he could spend time pondering the will of God.

Some of the seminarians thought he was making a mistake. Others, once they recovered from their shock, realized that he had thought it through thoroughly and, albeit difficult, made the correct decision for him. Matt Westcott said:

"I was not surprised to hear he was leaving; and, for what it's worth, I was not surprised when he told me he was coming back. I think leaving the seminary for a period of time was simply something he had to do to ensure he wasn't simply going with the flow of seminary life — a test he gave himself."

Dan asked all his friends at St. John's Seminary to keep him in their prayers.

Dan's leave of absence also startled Father Joseph Barranger, the Chaplain at Providence College during his undergraduate days and, who became his Spiritual Director prior to his entering St. John's Seminary. "When Dan called to inform me that he was leaving the seminary, I was shocked," Father Barranger later wrote to me, "but after listening to his explanation, I realized it was the right thing for him to do." He continued:

"It wasn't that he doubted his vocation. Diaconate Ordination was rapidly approaching. He was not convinced that he was mentally or spiritually prepared to proceed. If he were going to be a priest, he would be the best priest in the world. He would make no compromises; he would have to be able to give 100% to the priesthood."

Father Barranger knew Danny well both as a serious student, an accomplished athlete and someone well-grounded in his spiritual life. He had no doubt this young athlete would be all-in to run a good race for God. He remarked; "...undoubtedly, many angels were praying during Dan's discernment."

Father Brian Manning commented; "Every runner must run on his or her own. Father Dan struggled with knowing about his call but he kept running until he found the answer. The voice of God's call was hard to hear at one point for Father Dan but he ran and he listened until he heard clearly His blessed call to the Sacred Priesthood. We who were his family, mentors, and friends were part of the divine voice that called and cheered him on to service to our God."

As I discovered later, Jack knew about his brother's uncertainty but chose not to share that concern with Alice and me. When I learned, retrospectively, of their reticence in sharing such a tumultuous decision with us, I could understand they did not want to unnecessarily alarm us. Neither Alice nor I are hysterical or unreasonable and they knew we would be supportive of a well thought out decision yet there lingers in all of us a tendency to protect the ones we love from disappointments. I always preached to our kids that 'disappointment' should be applied first and foremost to self. It is easier to attribute perceived 'disappointment' to others than face the reality that it is 'self' is disappointed in 'self'. Apparently, I was ineffective in communicating this lesson of life to our kids.

Factored into his discernment dilemma was the impact of the negative impact on seminarians and other friends. "Apprehension about Mom and Dad's reaction was a huge concern and definitely exacerbated his dilemma," Jack recalled. "They were clearly pleased that he was in the seminary." Jack helped convince Danny "Mom and Dad would want him to make the decision which is right for him and they would be supportive."

When Danny told us of his decision we immediately told him we were 100% behind his rationale. He was relieved and told Alice and me; "It takes 'guts' to walk away from something you really love but on the chance I was blind to God's will I did what I thought I had to do to attain clarity".

In actuality Danny had no clue that Alice probably arrived at his need for clarity before he arrived at that conclusion. I was surprised, Alice was not.

Deep is the wisdom of the maternal heart.

Dan was always serious-minded about his faith. He was also a stubborn redhead never flinching from a fight and he would bring his ever-present battle readiness attitude to resolve the most important issue of his young life. Alice and I always prayed that our five children would seek the will of God. We had no doubt Dan would was striving to do just this. His conscience had convinced him the course he had charted required further clarity; his goal was to obtain clarity. This was the fight of his life, he was determined and he never backed away from a fight.

"May you fight a good fight by having faith and a good conscience. Some, by rejecting conscience, have made a shipwreck of their faith" (1 Timothy 1:18c-19).

Chapter 9: Leave of Absence

Relieve the troubles of my heart; bring me out of my distress.
(Psalm 25:17)

Dan's journey from the world of fun and frolic to the world of priestly preparation was influenced and navigated by prayers of the laity and clergy

Young Danny at the altar to hear Bishop Maguire's preaching.

As a young boy, Dan frequently exchanged correspondence with Bishop Joseph F. Maguire, Bishop of Springfield, who one day wrote, "I think that someday you will become a priest, Danny, but remember, it is between you and God." Those words truly guided his spiritual journey. Dan believed if he could establish a deep and personal friendship with Jesus Christ everything in his life would be in proper accord. I'm certain, with the utmost of confidence, that Dan devoted years of discernment to the care, custody, and control of Jesus Christ, who he truly believed was his closest friend.

At one point, when Dan was a young boy, Bishop Maguire enclosed his prayer card upon which is a poem, 'A Priest' which the bishop authored at the time of his ordination.

A PRIEST

I never could complain, Lord,
About my work for you.
I find delight and meaning
In the things a priest can do.

There is a joy in serving others
And sharing in their trials -
In quieting their heartaches
And quickening their smiles.

There is charity in listening
With a sympathetic ear
To distressed and lonely people
Who need someone just to hear.

There is peace in understanding
That your way, not mine, is best –
That when I've done my utmost,
Your grace will do the rest.

I am more convinced and certain
The longer, Lord, I live –
That every earnest priest receives
Much more than he can give.

And so my heart is grateful
For your goodness, Lord, to me.
A priest now and forever
Is all I wish to be.

~Bishop Joseph F. Maguire

More recently Dan read a book entitled, 'Maurice and Thérèse: The Story of a Love' by Bishop Patrick V. Ahern. Dan was moved by an exchange between St. Thérèse of Lisieux and a struggling seminarian friend of hers. Subsequently, he said, "I hope St. Thérèse is praying for this struggling seminarian, too." That was my first inclination that he too was struggling. Alice had 'read the tea leaves'; I had not.

Alice and I continued to pray during his protracted period of discernment, hoping it would be as easy for him as it had been for Saint John Paul II, who said:

"...At a certain point in my life, I became convinced that Christ was saying to me what he had said to me thousands of times before: 'Come, follow me!' There was a clear sense that what I heard in my heart was no human voice, nor was it just an idea of my own. Christ was calling me to serve him as a priest."

During this turbulent time in Dan's life, his family and his friends were united in support of his well-thought-out decision to take additional time for discernment. A few of his friends offered to introduce him to eligible young ladies but he wasted no time in setting them straight. His sole focus at this point in his life was figuring out God's plan for him; discernment was his new full-time job. Unfortunately, it came without a paycheck, so Dan also sat down with the Help Wanted ads and started networking among his broad acquaintanceship.

Upon leaving St. John's Seminary, Dan went into training, establishing a prayer and contemplation regimen. Daily Mass, Eucharistic Adoration, and three and a half years in the seminary had been extremely beneficial but, unfortunately, clarity on his vocation continued to be elusive. What was he missing? What needed to be addressed? When would he acquire resolution?

He re-entered the 'word a day world' with a part time job driving mourning cars in funeral processions for the Russell & Pica Funeral Home in Brockton. Dan met David Russell, a Funeral Director in Brockton on his first field assignment. Dan and Dave became good friends and Dave was first in line with an employment opportunity. Dan looked quite presentable in the good suits left over from his corporate life, but he did lack one necessity, a yarmulke. His first assignment was driving a mourning car in a Jewish funeral, and in courtesy to the family all funeral home personnel wore a yarmulke. Fortunately, Dave was able to provide Dan with proper attire.

Coincidentally, the destination of the Funeral Procession was a Jewish Cemetery in Brookline, abutting Brighton and Newton. The route to the cemetery in Brookline necessitated traveling along Commonwealth Ave in Boston and, past St. John's Seminary. As the procession proceeded slowly past the seminary, a faculty member paused in respect, did a double take, and then hustled back to the seminary to announce, "It's a good thing Kennedy's gone. I just saw him driving a limo in a Jewish funeral and, he's wearing a yarmulke."

Out of the blue, a Navy Commander from the Naval Chaplaincy School at the Newport Naval Base called to invite Dan to join the staff in the Chaplain School office. The Commander even offered the use of his condominium for three months, during which time he would be deployed on active duty. The condo was secluded on exclusive Goat Island, connected by causeway to beautiful Newport Harbor, and, within 'running' distance of the Naval Base.

Grateful and delighted with the opportunity to be associated with the religious arm of the Navy, Dan immediately accepted the offer and subsequently thanked Dave Russell for his generosity as he informed him that driving mourning cars were now in his 'rear view mirror.' Those months in Newport spent discerning God's will, were crucial in resolving Dan's dilemma. The officers and staff at the Naval College were extraordinarily supportive; many told him they thought he did have a priestly vocation, and they encouraged him to intensify his prayer time.

Winter snows did not impede his marathon training regimen. Regardless of snow, sleet, or freezing rain he could be seen running the shore route of Newport's inner harbor. In a sense he was in his comfort zone, just as he had trained on the shore of Scituate Harbor now his training was focused on the shore of Newport Harbor. He prayed as he ran, especially the Holy Rosary. On weekends when he visited his sister Katie he urged her to pray the Rosary about a concern she had, promising: "Mary works."

Eventually, the snow melted, spring arrived, and, on Patriots Day in April Dan ran, and finished, his sixth Boston Marathon. In his mind <u>finishing the race</u> was the litmus test; again, he attained his goal, he finished the race but did not achieve his secondary goal of completing the race the under 4 hours.

Shortly before the Commander was due to return from his deployment, a third job offer presented itself, again unsolicited. Alice and I were reminded of the old saying: *There's no coincidence, only Providence.* So many people, from a variety of backgrounds, seemed to be 'stepping up to the plate' and providing Dan with employment opportunities, and with opportunities to be in a prayerful environment. It was gratifying for him to receive a call from a Funeral Director friend, then a Navy Commander, and now a Senior Vice-President in the business world: Dick Kropp. All three, in their own way, were trying to help him during his ongoing struggle.

Dick Kropp, the Human Resource Senior Vice-President at the Cape Cod Hospital in Hyannis, MA was a parishioner at St. Mary of the Nativity in Scituate, MA. Dick learned that Dan was on a Leave of Absence from St. John's Seminary and he wanted to offer Dan a position in the Human Resource Department of the Cape Cod Hospital. In view of the fact that Dan was not technically fortified with the intricacies of a Human Resource Department he was peripherally familiar with most HR software programs from his time at Andersen Consulting and Cabot Corporation. Dick knew Dan as a bright young man with impeccable integrity, in his mind essential qualifications for a position in Human Resources.

When Dan's aunt, Judy, heard of the job opportunity in Hyannis she immediately offered Dan the use of her home in Centerville which abuts Hyannis and, with easy access to Cape Cod Hospital. Dan happily moved in. Here he was, just a few miles from his childhood summer home of frivolity in Dennisport, functioning in a business environment in Hyannis. He marveled at the contrast.

Cape Cod Hospital became a win-win for Dan. Not only was he remunerated for his work efforts, he could continue Marathon Training breathing in the brisk salt air on an ocean route around Hyannis Harbor plus, there was noontime Mass in the hospital chapel. Dan was in his natural habitat; running along the seashore plus; Mass, Eucharist Adoration, and gainful employment all under the same roof! *"My God will supply whatever you need."* (Philippians 4:19)

Day-by-day Dan prayed and contemplated, prayed and worked, prayed and ran, and day-by-day the clouds seem to disintegrate and clarity began to crystalize. At long last, as the sun was rising on the horizon off the shore of Hyannis, a sense of God's will for him also seemed to be crystalizing. *"When you seek me with all your heart, you will find me with you."* (Jeremiah 29:14)

The Folks at Home

Perhaps this is why he was away from you for a while, that you might have him back forever.
(Philemon 1:15)

Fully aware that Dan treasured his privacy, Alice and I never asked him whether he was considering a return to St. John's Seminary. Neither of us wanted to add to his tumultuous self-examination. Remaining silent was most difficult for Alice.

Of course, no mother ever stops worrying about her children. Alice was no exception. Nearly every day she asked me, "Do you think he'll go back to the seminary?" Before I could formulate a response, she would quickly continue, "I think he'll go back." A millisecond later, the litany continued; "Do you think he'll go back?" etc.

My answer, when I could finally squeeze it in, was always the same: "I don't know. I do know that he'll do the will of God whenever he figures it out."

Deep indeed is the wisdom of the maternal heart.

I was reminded of our old Baltimore Catechism lesson asking, "Why did God make you?" God made Dan to know Him, love Him, and serve Him in this world, and to be happy with Him forever in heaven. At age thirty-one Dan knew and loved God. He was just looking for clear instructions on the serving piece, and the happiness would take care of itself.

Dan told us that the Cape Cod Hospital Chaplain, a priest from the Diocese of Fall River celebrated a noontime Mass at the hospital chapel. Perceptively Dan said, "If this priest is doing his job, someday he'll ask if I've ever considered the possibility of a vocation."

Sure enough, one day, the Chaplain, Father John Murray popped the question, and when Dan said he was a former seminarian, Father Murray promptly invited him to lunch. It became a regular event, and the two became good friends. Father Murray was originally from Brockton, and they were both friends of the Funeral Director, Dave Russell. Forces for the good seemed to be in full array.

Springtime; A Life Altering Octave

Listen to the voice of the Lord your God...
(Jeremiah 26:13)

In May, Dan asked me if he could accompany me to the Archdiocese of Boston's Rite of Ordination at the Cathedral of the Holy

Cross. Several of Dan's seminary friends were being ordained to the Holy Priesthood and he wanted to attend the liturgy. For fear he would misconstrue the emotion I display at ordinations as remorse because he was on leave of absence I felt I should explain that I generally cry at ordinations. The beautiful Rite of Ordination, the fraternity of the priests assembled, and the presence of the Holy Spirit always overwhelm me, and invariably I cry with tears of joy. He was duly warned.

The Gospel Reading at the Rite of Ordination on that warm Saturday morning pertained to the rich young man who wanted to follow the Lord but couldn't relinquish his material possessions... *"he went away sad, for he had many possessions"* (Matthew 19:22b).

Cardinal Seán O'Malley's homily warmly commended the ordinandi for not turning away from following the Lord. Strangely, for the first time, I did not cry; Dan maintained the family tradition of weeping at an ordination. He was not just crying, he was bawling! No words were exchanged between us, during or after the ordination, pertaining to the tears but Cardinal Sean's powerful summation of the Gospel deeply affected Dan.

Newly ordained, Father David S. Marcham, invited us to a dinner reception at the Marriot Hotel in Quincy, MA, immediately following his ordination. When we arrived at the ordination reception I realized how uncomfortable Dan felt when he purposely selected a table in the extreme rear of the hall and selected a seat so he would be facing the wall with his back to the head table.

Soon his pal Matt Westcott, spotted us and blew his cover. Matt intentionally spoke loudly as he pointed toward Dan and said. "Mr. Kennedy, don't you think Cardinal Seán's homily was directed at him?" Embarrassed or perhaps abashed, Dan kept his head down in silence and applied himself to his meal. It was apparent that both Dan and Matt detected a correlation between the Gospel and Dan's leave of absence.

Certainly monetary deficiency continued to be a concern. The poverty of his life as a seminarian was chafing a bit. Dan had never been greedy; he was always generous to others but a chronic lack of income precipitated an unaccustomed self-denial.

As a serious athlete, Dan had always valued the importance of proper equipment and rigid adherence to an aggressive training program which enabled him to achieve his athletic goals. Similarly, a good salary from corporate America allowed him to indulge his appreciation of fine apparel, good workmanship, and the latest electronic innovation. Dan entered St. John's with a vast amount of golfing necessities; the latest clubs on the market, golf attire with latest logos, golf shoes for dry days, golf shoes for wet days, golf shoes with aluminum cleats, golf shoes with plastic cleats, tennis shoes, running shoes, walking shoes, dress shoes, baseball cleats, and all the gear required for a pick-up hockey game — not to mention his lifetime accumulation gadgets galore and kits for every situation. He had; tool kits, grilling kits, shaving kits, shoe shining kits, etc.

Taking pleasure in these belongings was hardly a blind passion for self-indulgent acquisition, however. Dan simply was living what Alice taught him long ago: Fixing broken items require proper tools and he had 'tools' for almost any occasion. In any event, diocesan priests do not take the vow of poverty, so I dismissed the possible abandonment of his hobbies as a concern of his.

Father David also invited Dan to be an usher at his First Mass of Thanksgiving in Sacred Heart Church in Quincy and he was pleased to participate. Dan's primary responsibility was to wear a business suit and stand at the front door of the church to greet guests, hand out programs and escort people to their seats.

After Alice and I were seated we turned to view Father Dave process down the center aisle we were astonished to see Dan, leading the procession! He was not in his business suit, he was wearing an alb (much too short) and holding high the crucifix! As we learned later, a seminarian who had been scheduled to serve at the Mass was marooned in a traffic delay so, on the spot, Father Dave thought of Dan as a substitute acolyte and, Father Farren, the Rector of St. John's Seminary, who was in attendance for the First Mass, concurred. Although Dan, the former athlete, was never a 'designated hitter', surprisingly he became 'designated draftee of the day'.

How strange yet familiar it must have felt for Dan to wear an alb again and process with clergy into the sanctuary. We were grateful that Father Farren, in a sense, expunged our struggling son from his self-imposed exile.

The following Saturday, eight days after attending the Rite of Ordination at the Cathedral of the Holy Cross in Boston, Dan attended another Rite of Ordination at the Cathedral of St. Joseph in Manchester, New Hampshire. Dan was honored when his seminary pal, Jeff Statz invited him to be a Lector at his ordination for the Diocese of Manchester. Father Jeff wrote later:

"In many ways my journey to priesthood came with more ease than Dan's, but what impressed me most about Dan was his courage to follow God's calling. I remember him telling me that he wanted to make sure that this was truly a calling from God. He didn't want it to be just something

that he wanted, but an authentic invitation from Christ him-self."

"Dan showed us that to follow Jesus and walk in His way means picking up the cross each day with courage, but also with joy. It is a joy only Christ can give to those who enter into His life. In His love God revealed this to Dan."

After the ordination, the Bishop of Manchester commended Dan on his proclamation of the Reading which he said was 'superb'. At that point the bishop urged him to consider becoming a Lector in his home parish. Dan politely thanked him but did not mention his years of public speaking and seminary training.

A Labor of Love

Pray without ceasing.
(1 Thessalonians 5:17)

Priests and laity alike were praying for Dan during a frigid winter and a much-awaited spring. Often Dan's friends mentioned that they felt certain that he had a vocation to the priesthood. Stubbornly independent, though, Dan resolved to solicit another view, and, as learned later, another perspective came from his friend Billy Condron.

Dan and Billy met occasionally for dinner and to share a few laughs. Billy recalled:

"Over dinner, we talked often about Danny's choice to become a priest. He was completely candid about the internal battle he was having between the life he had chosen and the one he had given up. Certainly it was a difficult time in

the Church's history, and one could argue that St. John's Seminary was ground zero for the devastating abuse scandal that rocked the Roman Catholic Church."

"Danny struggled with being painted with a brush stained with an impropriety he didn't deserve. At times, this galvanized his resolve. However, it also caused him to question a choice that was already fraught with trade-offs and sacrifices. No one will ever know how he would have marinated in the cauldron that was seminary life if the fires of scandal had not been ever present. But I do know it made a fragile, painstaking decision that much more challenging."

When Dan called and asked Billy to play devil's advocate, Billy did his best for his longtime pal:

"He was trying to come to a decision on his future and felt he had heard the case for returning to the priesthood from various friends and confidants. He told me he wanted to hear the other side of the argument — the rationale for living his life as a layman."

"As I reflect now, I am struck by the clear-eyed purpose behind our discussion that night. Danny was making a monumental decision — the largest a man can make and one so permanent and far-reaching that many men avoid the deliberation altogether. Not Danny. He was too courageous to skirt the questions and too intelligent to blindly follow a path for which he wasn't fully committed."

"So we talked. I spoke about what an amazing husband and father he would be. That his success in any career was a given, considering his intellect and work ethic. We spoke honestly of the sacrifices he would be making, of giving up the emotional intimacy available in a strong Catholic marriage, of his desire to be a good parent in the way his Mom and Dad had been to him."

"The conversation lasted for hours. Danny never committed one way or another throughout the night. He just listened and took it all in. We ended as we always did, with a hug and a promise to get together again soon."

A few days later Dan called Billy to say he had not been sufficiently persuasive. Dan had decided to return to St. John's.

"I was thrilled for him," Billy recalls, "because I knew he had made the choice with a resolve born out of a fierce discernment." Billy rejoiced that his friend had found the comfort of certainty and the joy of knowing he was on the right path at last.

Ask and Ye Shall Receive.

You, O Lord, know me, you see me, you have found at heart I am with you. (Jeremiah 12: 1-3)

In early July on our back porch Dennisport, Dan informed Alice and me that he had applied to re-enter St. John's Seminary. I expressed support and pleasure, Alice was ecstatic! Her concerns had been allayed and her prayers answered, indeed, 'A Mother's Love is a Blessing'.

Dan explained how important it was for him to clearly discern the will of God before taking the vows of ordination, adding that "it took guts" to ask for a leave of absence but that he needed to do that. We agreed and praised him, assuring him that we understood the difficult discernment he endured. I think he was relieved we had managed not to pressure him in either direction, trusting in Christ to work things out between them.

Although he did receive unofficial encouragement that his application had been well received, the month of July went by with no official response. The month of August came and went and still he was not 'officially' back on board.

Impatient yet resigned to one more test, Dan held his temper in check and awaited notification of approval. Remembering his rejection by Notre Dame, I felt some apprehension. Surely St. John's Seminary would not turn him down, would they?

At last, just three days before classes convened in September 2005, Cardinal Seán O'Malley telephoned to say Dan's application had been approved. "Welcome back to St. John's Seminary," the Cardinal told him. All Alice and I could say was, "Deo gratias!"

For Dan, the time away from the seminary had been necessary. "God wants happy priests, not uncertain priests," he said. Dan was always blessed with a *gift of happiness*, and over the next two years Alice and I continued to see his inner joy increase as he progressed closer toward Holy Orders. We were convinced that Dan would be a happy priest.

Chapter 10: Homecoming

I sought the Lord, and he answered me, delivered me from all my fears.
(Psalm 34:5)

When classes convened at St. John's Seminary in September 2005, Dan was pleased to receive a warm reception. Brother seminarians, administrators and faculty members alike came up to shake his hand and sincerely say, "Welcome back, Dan," and "Welcome home." Quite likely they wondered if some particular thing had given him conviction and clarity, but not even his close friend Matt Westcott knew. Matt said:

> *"Dan always played his cards close to his vest. I had the feeling that his leaving was really a pause, not a stop and restart; hence my lack of surprise at his leaving and his return. I think he simply gave himself time off of the treadmill and was able to refocus and revise himself — like taking a water break on a long run."*

Those who knew Dan well realized that he spent his time away from SJS diligently praying for clarity augmented by Eucharist Adoration, Confession, contemplation and introspection. Whatever route he decided to run his seminarian brothers were in support of him. They were exceedingly happy he chose the path to priesthood.

They were also happy because it was just plain fun to have him around. His infectious laugh, his lively, boisterous teasing, interspersed with deep dives into serious topics, had been missed. Since his first year, anyone who challenged Dan on a point, from sports to theology to craft beers, learned to expect a vigorous defense. In fact, one rebuttal was legendary — the time he tackled and pinned a condescending upperclassman who liked to sneer at questions he deemed naïve. Dan strongly suggested that this man find a better way to assist his younger brethren.

He himself was a model for others. Father Mark Murphy recalls:

"Dan was a tremendous support and example to me as I was just starting out in my formation to become a priest of the Archdiocese of Boston. At formal and informal seminarian gatherings Dan would always spend time with me just to shoot the breeze or to answer any questions I might have."

The give and take outside of class included dreadful puns and corny jokes, Dan's milieu. As he settled in again to classwork and the daily routine, Dan realized how much he missed the companionship of these friends and their shared spiritual journey. With the enrollment still in free fall there remained an undercurrent of pessimism yet; for the most part seminarians seemed to have kept their eye on the ball.

In 2005, the Archdiocesan newspaper, *The Pilot,* interviewed several seminarians in an effort to encourage vocations; Dan was among those selected to offer a contribution to the article. When asked his favorite Biblical passage, Dan responded, "'be still and know that I am God'" (Psalm 46). I was surprised to read his observation in *The Pilot*, as I still thought of my son as operating with a high level of intensity, always active, 24/7. Then it dawned on me: Dan was settling into his new mode of prayerful obedience to God's will, which meant breaking his lifelong habit of racing ahead and leading the charge.

It wasn't long before Dan was back on the speaking circuit, representing St. John's Seminary in promoting vocations at parishes throughout the region. In October he traveled to Washington, D.C. for the Marine Corps Marathon, running his best pace ever. Although he achieved his goal of finishing the race he fell short of attaining his secondary objective; breaking the 4-hour mark.

Dan enjoyed seeing the eager anticipation demonstrated by the seminarians of the Class of 2006 (his former class) as they were anxiously preparing to take diaconate vows in January as Transitional Deacons; one step away from priestly ordination in May. Their excitement permeated the entire seminary. Dan would have been among them if not for his supplemental discernment time; but I saw no signs of regret, just contentment.

By tradition, there is a St. John's Seminary 'Deacon Night' during the month of May when Transitional Deacons are "roasted" by the following years 'Class' of seminarians. Dan 'bridged' both classes so he was a natural to be selected for 2006 Deacon Night Committee. Dan surreptitiously contacted family and friends of each deacon to gather background material and old pictures which would be captioned with comical remarks. By the end of the evening the men were well and thoroughly "roasted," peppered with jokes, and stuffed with happy memories. Camaraderie personified.

Welcome Back to Scituate Harbor

Once more will he fill your mouth with laughter and your lips with rejoicing. (Job 8:21)

As Dan settled back into seminary life, he requested to be re-assigned to St. Mary of the Nativity in Scituate, where he enjoyed serving during the summer of 2004. He also looked forward to renewing friendships with parishioners, especially Dick Kropp, his boss at the Cape Cod Hospital. It was Dick Kropp who sought him out during his leave of absence and offered him a position at the Cape Cod Hospital; a heavenly haven during his time of trial.

Another bonus of St. Mary of the Nativity was the pure joy of living on the shore of beautiful Scituate Harbor. After his sixth Boston Marathon in April, Dan was contemplating running in another Marine Corps Marathon in the Fall of 2006, and he loved being able to train on a coastal route. He often said the silence of running stilled his mind; it was a private time with the Lord — and with Our Lady, for he often used the time to pray the Rosary.

The young parishioners were especially happy to welcome Dan back, remembering his sense of humor and enthusiasm. The CCD and Confirmation Class realized that he was genuinely interested in their spiritual development and cared about their progress. Dan discovered that teaching them about Christ was deeply rewarding, and their directness and honesty delighted him. "What's this fear of the Lord stuff, anyhow?" they demanded. "Who wants to be afraid?" Dan rose to every challenge his students posed, uplifting them in response. He also thought that his niece Ashley might benefit from attending a class or two to experience the CCD program at St. Mary's.

Danny possessed an intense love for Ashley. He was constantly looking for opportunities to help her or, to tease her. Often used teasing as a means to communicate a life's lesson to her. He was a wonderful uncle.

No matter where he was or what he was scheduled to do he would find a way to allocate time to be home to carve a Halloween

Pumpkin for Ashley. He also insisted on purchasing the 'perfect pumpkin' so he could carve the most ferocious image imaginable. He even came equipped with his own personal 'pumpkin carving kit'. I think he enjoyed the finished product as much as or, more than, Ashley. He was a 'big kid' at heart.

Once Uncle Dan invited Ashley to join him and the CCD kids for supper at St. Mary's — not telling her it would be a "Hunger Banquet." The event is a popular way to compare first-world economics with third-world poverty; this visual enactment was new to Ashley and to Dan's CCD students.

Dan divided the students into three groups. A select few enjoyed a spacious area with tablecloths, silverware, and china; waiters brought them chicken, pizza, and corn on the cob, apples, cake and ice cream for dessert. Off to the side, a larger group was seated in chairs; they did not have a table. Their utensils were limited to one spoon in order to eat, one boiled egg, drink one small glass of juice, and one cookie. Meanwhile a crowd of students sat jammed together on the bare floor each with no utensils or plates' just one small cup of water, a crust of bread, and a small scoop of rice.

The lesson was vivid: in the first world countries 'our daily bread' provides far more sustenance than second or third world countries. Once Ashley recovered from her initial annoyance of being assigned to the third world group she benefited from the practical dramatization of the world economy. Dan and Ashley liked to tease each other so she initially felt Uncle Dan deliberately assigned her to the third world group to tease her, to an extent, she was right but his intent was to provide her with an insight into 'how the other half lives'. Teasing was a vehicle in which Dan communicated life lessons and, his unconditional love to Ashley.

As Dan wrote to her years later:

"I am not sure you know how important you are to me. You have always been a gift from God to our family. Sometimes teasing is how I show my love for you…. Ashley, it is so important that you stay close to Jesus, by saying your prayers and going to Mass. Jesus loves you even more than your uncle Danny. I love you, kid!"

St. Mary of the Nativity pastor, Father Brian Manning, realized in their first summer together in Scituate, Dan's winning personality and clear passion for Christ. In order to prepare him to be an effective Parochial Vicar he provided him with a wide range of opportunities for firsthand experience. As a pastoral supervisor during Dan's diaconal year, Father Manning mandated that Dan become involved in all aspects of parish life; from participating on the Parish Council to serving on the Cemetery Commission. If there were a parish school he would have been on the Board of Education. "Dan possessed inner strength and determination," Father Brian recalled. "Dan also took seriously the demands of preparation. He trained hard to be a priest; over time we became good friends."

Dan, in turn, was grateful for his supervisor's spiritual guidance, sound advice, and priestly example. Much about being a good priest simply cannot be taught in a classroom.

Transitional Deacon

I continue my pursuit toward the goal, the prize of God's upward calling, in Christ Jesus. (Philippians 3:14)

In January 2007, to mark the fifth anniversary of the clergy scandal exposé, the Boston Globe interviewed seminarians including "Dan Kennedy, a solidly built young man with a reddish crew cut and chiseled features." Dan told the reporter, "This ordeal, which all Catholics are enduring because of a few criminal priests, has proven to me to be affirmation that I do have a vocation to the priesthood." Bearing the shame of the clergy scandal strengthened those seminarians who survived.

Ordained ministry has three ranks: Permanent Deacon, Transitional Deacon, and Priest (including Bishops). The permanent diaconate is for men (typically married) who do not plan to become priests; transitional diaconate is the step in Holy Orders which immediately precedes priestly ordination. A deacon may officiate at baptisms, marriages, funeral and burial services. They may distribute Holy Communion and preach homilies. In Boston, seminarians are ordained to the Transitional Diaconate in the month of January, typically, four months prior to the Rite of Ordination to the Holy Priesthood which is held typically during the month of May.

Matt Westcott, who ordained a Transitional Deacon on the same day as Dan, January 27, 2007, points out another aspect of the diaconate: "It is at the transitional diaconate that a man promises celibacy, not at the Rite of Ordination to the Holy Priesthood.

So, the permanence of that transitional diaconate commitment looms large."

Dan felt that forgoing a wife and children in order to fully commit to serving the Lord was a rational sacrifice. St. Paul's advice made perfect sense to him:

> "I should like you to be free of anxieties. An unmarried man is anxious about the things of the Lord, how he may please the Lord. But a married man is anxious about the things of the world, how he may please his wife." (1 Corinthians 7:32-33)

When Dan embraced the vow of celibacy, foregoing the prospect of a wife and children, he did so in order to be free to nurture and guide every child of God in need of spiritual care.

During Christmas season in 2006, I wondered if Dan felt some trepidation about his impending diaconate ordination. He seemed buoyant as usual, attending various Christmas family gatherings, delighting in decorating the Christmas tree as was his annual desire but, sporadically, he seemed somewhat subdued. I added to my daily prayers an extra plea that the Lord would give Dan the grace to persevere.

I felt somewhat relieved when, on the morning of the Diaconate Ordination, Father Jim DiPerri, a priest in the archdiocese, came over to Alice and me as we sat in our pew at the Cathedral of the Holy Cross and told us, "Don't worry, he'll be fine." He had just prayed with Dan in the sacristy of the cathedral, and he assured us all was well.

In a beautiful ceremony, Cardinal Seán O'Malley ordained seven men from Boston to the Transitional Diaconate comparing them to the original Seven Deacons elected by the early Christian Church and referring to them as 'the Magnificent Seven'. Each of the newly ordained deacons was presented with the Book of the Gospels. Father Brian Manning, who vested Deacon Dan, wasted no time in putting him to work: Dan was scheduled to assist at Mass and proclaim the Gospel for the first time that afternoon at St. Mary of the Nativity, in Scituate Harbor.

The Ordination to the Diaconate took place on January 27, 2007, exactly one year before Father Dan's passing.

Later that day, at St. Mary of the Nativity's 4:00 p.m. Mass for the first time Deacon Dan ascended the pulpit to proclaim the Gospel and deliver his first Homily. His words were tailored for the parish that had helped teach him how to serve God. Deacon Dan said that when his brother Jackie asked what he hoped to accomplish as a deacon and a prospective priest he replied, "I hope to convince people of the relevance of Christ in their lives."

By "convince" did this champion debater mean dry logic and cold facts? Not at all. He meant a personal experience of Christ's friendship — the priceless gift that had transformed him from a white-collar corporate "suit" to a white-collar clergyman.

After Mass, Father Brian hosted a reception and dinner at the rectory for our family and a small group of Deacon Dan's friends, including Dick Kropp and his wife as well as Rosemary Lonborg and her husband, Jim Lonborg the former Major League Baseball Cy Young Award winner in 1967. A highlight of the festivities for Deacon Dan was Jim's gracious offer to allow him to wear Jim's Boston Red Sox 2004 World Series Ring! Fitting in that, after an 86-year famine, Seminarian Dan celebrated the Boston Red Sox

2004 World Series victory by purportedly ringing the bells of St. John's Seminary.

There was no Boston Marathon for Dan in 2007. For once he realized his plate was full. Prayerful preparation for his impending ordination precluded running the 2007 Boston Marathon. Justification for breaking his streak of consecutive marathons was mitigated in that he could commence a new streak beginning with the 2008 Boston Marathon. In hindsight, he was wrong! As Father Brian wrote later, our son was drawing near a more important finish line:

"Running a marathon is in the midst of many, but it is in many ways done alone. Each runner must run on his or her own. Father Dan struggled with knowing about his call, but he kept running until he found the answer. The voice of God's call was hard to hear at one point for Father Dan, but he ran and listened until he heard clearly his blessed call to the Sacred Priesthood. We who were his family, mentors and friends, were part of the divine voice that called and cheered him on to service to our God."

Supervising interns can be hard work, but for Father Manning working with this "great marathoner" had been a pleasure. "I was graced to be a helper and cheerer of Dan along his path to the priesthood," Father Manning said, and he looked forward to embracing him as a fellow priest in May.

Sing A New Song for the Lord

Then our mouths were filled with laughter; our tongues sang for joy. (Psalm 126:2)

As spring spruced-up Scituate Harbor in 2007, Father Manning informed Deacon Dan that he expected him to sing the lengthy, soaring Exultet at St. Mary's Easter Vigil. This Easter Proclamation, chanted a cappella, celebrates the end of darkness and joy of the fresh-kindled Paschal light, must be loudly and forcefully proclaimed — and the prospect struck fear into Dan's heart. Even though he was multi-talented, singing was definitely not one of his talents!

Despite coaching over the years from fellow seminarians, Dan's singing voice remained an embarrassing monotone. But as with other endeavors he wanted to master, Deacon Dan was not ashamed to seek professional help, so he asked Director of Music at St. John's Seminary to train him to chant the Exultet.

As Holy Week rapidly approached, it was obvious to the Director of Music that Deacon Dan was incapable of chanting the Exultet at the Easter Vigil. When he called Father Manning to convey the Director of Music's disapproval, Father Manning was unmoved. "Good, bad, or indifferent: you will sing," was his reply. In desperation, Deacon Dan begged Deacon "Broadway Bob" Blaney for some last-minute lessons as the Triduum was looming on the horizon.

At Deacon Dan's invitation, Alice and I attended the Easter Vigil Mass at St. Mary of the Nativity We were fully aware of the weeks of trauma he endured in an unsuccessful attempt to acquire vocal skills. As the procession proceeded down the center aisle of the darkened church, a jubilant, a cappella voice reverberated: "Exsultet jam!" Let them rejoice now! Neither of us recognized the warm, confident voice of the cantor; pessimists that we are, we assumed Dan had found a last minute replacement. But slowly the light passing from candle to candle brightened the darkness, much to our astonishment we recognized the cantor: our son Deacon Dan!

Of course we were proud and moved — and as usual with a beautiful ritual, there were tears of joy in my eyes. Later we learned that Father Brian was also deeply pleased with Dan's efforts. His newly ordained deacon mastered the two-part lesson variously attributed to St. Augustine and St. Ignatius of Loyola: *"Pray as if everything depends on God, and work as if everything depends on you."*

Seminary Alum; Preparatory Program Fulfilled

"Here I am," I said, "send me!" (Isaiah 6:8)

As May 2007 drew near and with it Dan's priestly ordination, I thought back on how he had come to this point. From kindergarten through college, he attended Catholic institutions and acquired basic knowledge of the faith to spiritually fortify him in surviving in a secular society. Growing up he was blessed to know many priests and religious whom he observed, admired, and, ultimately, imitated. Those years of preparation came together at St. John's Seminary, which grounded him with in-depth theology needed to defend the faith and provided pastoral skills required of a Roman Catholic priest.

Always a confident public speaker, Deacon Dan successfully completed St. John's Seminary's priest preparatory program where, in addition to a deep spirituality fortified his pastoral and catechistical skills. As they say in Human Resource circles, he repurposed his skillset to enhance his addressable market; or as they said at the Corrib Pub, "When Dan's telling a tale, everyone wants to listen."

Each of Deacon Dan's Seminarian Field Assignments was a blessing. In every setting, he met field supervisors who assisted him in finding Christ in others. He always had the joy of Christ in his heart and now he could better share that joy with others. He also made lasting friendships with dozens of parishioners and staff members throughout the archdiocese who challenged, encouraged, and warmly supported him.

Deacon Dan's excitement was evident as the date of ordination drew near, but he did not neglect his academic responsibilities. After his final exam, typical of his high spirits, he marked the closure of his time at St. John's Seminary by sending out a cryptic and succinct email: "IT IS FINISHED!" Alice and I thought that a bit irreverent, but saying goodbye to the classroom must have felt like a taking a significant stride closer to heaven. His email brevity was a forerunner to the world of today; texting cryptic and abbreviated messages.

Our family prepared for the ordination in various ways. Alice decided we needed new kitchen cabinets to celebrate properly. Deacon Dan discovered a newly marketed flexible golf club which was quickly residing in the trunk of his car. Alice and the girls went shopping for new outfits from head to toe. As for me, I just paid the bills.

Alice also put in a surprising amount of time discussing arrangements for the post-ordination reception at the Weston Golf

Club, which was facilitated by Deacon Dan's friend Patrick Murphy's membership. Deacon Dan also prevailed upon us to accept David Russell's gracious offer of chauffeured limousines, reassuring his mother that no funeral accouterments would appear.

Planning the ordination reception entailed coordinating numerous foreseen and unforeseen details; Alice's forte. The newly ordained deacon was pre-occupied with designing a custom made Chalice, developing an invitation list and formulating a speaker program.

Deacon Dan told me he planned to ask people to speak who had most impacted him at various stages of his life. That list included his brother Jackie; his high school language instructor and forensics coach, Brother Anthony Cavet, CPC; and the Pastor of St. Mary of the Nativity, Father Brian Manning.

When I said it would be an honor to introduce him, the red-headed ordinandi shook his head; "No." Mike Rush had already volunteered. I retorted, "I would like to introduce you." Again, Deacon Dan demurred.

After all those years of parenting and prayer, not to mention numerous drives to and from cold hockey rinks, purchasing equipment and lacing skates, I hadn't made the cut?

Listen Dan," I asserted, "the only part I want to play in your ordination weekend is to introduce you!" Sensing the tone of my voice he realized the importance I attached to speaking. At that point he agreed, I could introduce him and we sealed the deal with his traditional bone-crushing Kennedy handshake and a hug of reconciliation.

I was pleased that he eventually acceded as I had contemplating bringing out the heavy artillery, the Kennedy Family Fourth

Commandment: Honor thy father and thy mother. On the other hand that strategy may not have succeeded; he may have had to choose between father and mother. It is entirely possible Alice expressed her reluctance to have Danny include me on the roster of speakers. Alice and I have been blessed with years of a loving relationship but, she seems to believe that my emotional proclivity would likely come to the forefront in a public setting and embarrass myself. At any rate, Danny and I amicably resolved the issue: I would introduce him at the reception.

A week before his ordination, Danny and I enjoyed breakfast together at a local restaurant. As soon as we began to sip our coffee he looked at me intently and said; "Dad, I intend to be good at this!" I had been rolling my eyes at his usual starving athlete's meal of three eggs, sausage, bacon, hash browns, and toast, but I sat up straight when I heard his emphatic remark, thinking, "What a powerful statement; what a great outlook." Dan was determined to become the best priest he could possibly be! Amen.

As I continued to marvel at his determination and, his insatiable appetite, he proceeded to present me with two assignments. First, he wanted me to purchase an inexpensive purple stole from the Sister Disciples of the Divine Master in Downtown Boston. Father Dan proceeded to explain that he would wear the stole the first time he heard a confession, then he would return the stole to me for safekeeping. Secondly; after the ordination he would give me the linen cloth used to dry his hands of the chrism oil. He suggested that I place the stole and the linen cloth in our safe deposit box.

"What's that all about?" I asked, and Danny explained that it was a tradition among seminarians. After our deaths, the stole should be placed in my casket and the linen cloth placed in Alice's casket. I was moved by this forethought, and for a second I even pictured Dan presiding at my funeral. Who could have guessed how differently things would turn out?

The seven ordinandi from the Archdiocese of Boston spent the week prior to the ordination on Retreat in preparation for their lives as 'a priest forever'. When they returned from the Retreat they were invited to dinner with the Archbishop of Boston, Cardinal Seán O'Malley on the Friday night before the ordination. During the informal dinner, Cardinal Seán informed them of their first priestly assignment.

Every man in the Class of 2007 was eager to learn where they would reside for the next three years. Deacon Dan was thrilled when Cardinal Seán informed him that he had been assigned Parochial Vicar at St. John the Evangelist Parish in Winthrop, MA on Boston Harbor. Another seaside assignment! As soon as he had an opportunity, Deacon Dan was on the phone to introduce himself to the pastor Father Charlie Bourke.

Amazingly, Father Bourke remembered Deacon Dan from a family funeral a few years previously. Father Bourke's cousin Larry McCarthy had been one of several lapsed Catholics chided, challenged and charmed by the red-haired bouncer at the Corrib Pub. When Larry died, Deacon Dan was amongst the mourners.

Deacon Dan told Father Bourke he was looking forward to meeting the parishioners and to settling in his own room. Father Bourke responded that it was a great time to be joining the parish as St. John the Evangelist was celebrating their Centennial Year, he did however caution him that it would be several weeks before his accommodations would be available. Deacon Dan said he would be completely happy as long as he could look forward to some home cooked Italian meals as there is a large Italian population in Winthrop and, need I say, Deacon Dan *loved* Italian food.

PART THREE: FATHER DAN

Chapter 11: Rite of Ordination

"Like Melchizedek you are a priest forever." (Psalm 110:4)

Saturday, May 26, 2007, dawned a perfect spring day, with blue skies, chirping birds, blossoming trees, and flowers in bloom. Nervous anticipation ruled at 45 Woodlawn Avenue, where the aunts and uncles joined us to await the arrival of the Russell & Pica Limousine. The ladies were still admiring one another's outfits when the limousine arrived; soon everyone was comfortable in the confines of a luxurious limousine. Destination: The Cathedral of the Holy Cross in Boston.

Family and friends of the seven ordinandi crowded into the beautiful cathedral, where the stained glass windows were radiant with streaming sunlight. All rose eagerly as the choir began "This Is the Feast of Victory for Our God," and a seemingly endless line of ecstatic bishops and priests entered the historic edifice followed by the seven ordinandi and Cardinal Seán Patrick O'Malley.

The Rite of Ordination was spectacular! Every hymn of thanksgiving reverberated with a glorious crescendo every prayer a profound communication with our heavenly father and the congregant's response enthusiastically emitting tearful acclaim.

The Cardinal's homily reminded us how the Church forms a holy family. Together we stand in the presence of God our Father, under the loving eye of Mary our Mother, while all these sons and brothers, God's holy priests, through the power of the Holy Spirit bring us the living Christ, our Savior. Consecrated clergy, young and old form a fraternity with an unbroken lineage stretching back to the first apostles; those fallible and holy friends of Jesus, Our Lord.

Deacon Dan was the picture of humility as Cardinal Seán anointed his hands with the holy chrism oil and kissed his newly blessed hands. Tears welled in Father Dan's eyes as he tried to contemplate the transformation of his heart and soul. Cardinal Seán laid his hands on each of the ordinandi, and, before our very eyes, the Holy Spirit transformed them into men who can stand *in persona Christi* (in the person of Christ). Each of the ordinandi received all the powers and graces reserved for ordained priests — to offer Mass, to give us Christ Himself in the Eucharist, to bring us Christ's forgiveness in confession, to bear Christ's healing in the anointment of the sick, and to bring us all to better understand and practice the Gospel of Christ.

The manifestation of the Holy Spirit was obvious as priest after priest ascended the steps of the Sanctuary to 'lay hands' on their newly consecrated brothers. Alice and I were moved to think how blessed we were to witness our son become a part of this ancient tradition, which stretches back over centuries. Young and old, these men devoted their lives to Christ's Holy Bride, the Catholic Church. Young and old, they were equally brothers of Our Lord Jesus Christ.

The humility and pride Alice and I felt as our son received the sacrament of holy orders left us speechless. Our boy, with all his faults and failings — a sinner like ourselves — had been called by the Lord to serve His people. He had strained to hear that still, small voice, and then raced with joy to answer the summons.

Our stubborn, independent, redhead vowed obedience to his bishop. Our proud, strong athlete lay down, prostrate on the Altar in submission and humility. Our little boy was now *in persona Christi*!

At his First Mass at St. Mary's of the Nativity, Father Dan would recall that moment:

"Last Saturday at the ordination, I committed my life to Christ's Church forever. The ceremony involved my classmates and me actually lying down on the floor of the cathedral, an action that symbolizes our unworthiness for the office we assume and our dependence upon God and the prayers of the Christian community. It has been said that one has never stood so tall as when he lies prostrate before our Lord."

Tears of joy were glistening on Alice's cheeks. Our little redheaded Altar Server was *"a priest forever, according to the order of Melchizedek."*

The Archbishop of Boston, Cardinal Seán O'Malley knelt before each of the newly ordained priests to receive from each his first priestly blessing. Processing down the center aisle, the newest priests smiled from ear to ear, and all around them faces beamed with gladness and gratitude. The Cathedral seemed to shine with a holy light.

The new "Father" meets his mother Alice.

Afterwards, families clustered at the steps to the sanctuary. No matter what the occasion nothing is complete until sufficient pictures have been taken. Many people lingered as well to receive blessings from Father Dan Kennedy, Father Matt Westcott, and the other new priests. Some did so for the charming tradition that a priest's first blessings carry "extra" grace. Others did so as a reality check, confirming the truth that the brother they had teased and fought with for decades was now consecrated to God and inarguably deserved their respect.

An elderly lady at the edge of the crowd was gently shaking her head in amazement and amusement. In her eyes, I thought, one of these priests must also have been a young rascal who has become 'a priest forever'.

Father Dan blesses his parents!

Come to the Table of Plenty

A feast is made for merriment and wine gives joy to the living. (Ecclesiastes 10:19a)

The Saturday evening Ordination Reception Dinner reception at the Weston Golf Club was hours away, so some relatives and a few close friends gathered at our home in Needham to rejoice as a family. Over and over we heard; "Hi 'Father' Dan" no one tired of using his new title and his grin reflected his delight at hearing those words. In deference to his visitors and, in respect to the awesome occasion, Father Dan reserved his favorite bone-crushing handshake for another occasion.

Father Dan's pals and cousins were treated to a demonstration of his newest golfing gadget. At our lawn party Father Dan was the center of attention, not because he was a newly ordained priest but because 'the new priest' was demonstrating a collapsible golf iron that just came on the market! The iron possessed a hinged, collapsible shaft which automatically uncoupled during a 'flawed' golf swing. If the golfer's swing was smooth and executed at an appropriate speed the iron would not uncouple. Typical, Father Dan managed to acquire the latest 'toy' on the market! He justified purchasing this toy in preparation for the week vacation he was taking with Father Matt Westcott at the Mount Stratton Golf Academy in Vermont.

Naturally his cousins teased him for selecting such a secular getaway, but Father Dan cheerfully cited his parochial assignment as justification. St. John the Evangelist supports its Youth Ministry with the proceeds of an annual golf tournament at the Winthrop County Club. Consequently, it was important that the new Parochial Vicar hone his golfing skills before August, for the good of the parish, right?

As always, Father Dan's goal was to excel and he was certain that a personal coach would enhance the probability of fulfilling that expectation. Later, however, he was much abashed. After inviting Alice and I to play in the St. John the Evangelist Golf Tournament we witnessed the 'fruits' of his summer instruction! Father Dan proceeded to slice tee shots into the woods and hook his fairway irons into the water. It's a sad but true admission among golfers: Pride goeth before the ball.

For the second time in one day, Dave Russell's limousines pulled up in front of our home and Alice and I were soon in route to join more family and friends at the ordination reception at the Weston

Golf Club. Father Dan's good friend, Patrick Murphy had graciously sponsored the venue for a truly, elegant affair. Family from both sides of Father Dan's genealogical ancestry, the maternal Haggerty clan and the paternal Kennedy clan were in attendance to welcome our collective families' first priest.

Father Dan designed his own chalice, which was on display at the reception. The cup is silver, with red strip on the stem in honor his formation by the Irish Christian Brothers of Catholic Memorial High School whose school colors are silver and red. The chalice was a gift to Father Dan from Mom and Dad. The Chalice was inscribed with; the date of ordination, May 26, 2007, and, "In Memory of the Haggerty and Kennedy Families."

It is interesting in that, May 26th, is the Feast Day of St. Philip Neri who was noted for an ever-present sense of humor which enabled him to capture the attention of listeners as he subsequently presented a spiritual message to receptive ears. St Philip was said to possess a 'playful humor with a shrewd wit'. "A joyful heart is more easily made perfect than a downcast one". Similarity?

Father Manning was an essential contributor as a featured speaker when he said; "Running a Marathon in the midst of many is, in a way, a route traveled alone by each runner. The voices of many were cheering him on but Father Dan was running 'alone' struggling to hear the voice of God's call. He ran and he listened until he heard clearly the divine voice call him to the Sacred Priesthood."

The Ordination Reception would not have been complete without a brief remark from his longtime friend, Massachusetts State Representative, Michael F. Rush who said; "Danny was the epitome of our high school motto, Vince in Bono Malum, "Conquer Evil by Doing Good". As a high school student, college student, and as a priest, Father Dan was and will continue to be fiercely loyal to his family, friends, and to his Faith. People are excited and inspired that a young man with such intense spirituality, extraordinary personality, unbridled energy, and unwavering and upbeat attitude has been ordained to the Holy Priesthood."

Richie Gormley, another one of Father Dan's many West Roxbury friends insisted on engaging Andy Healey's Irish Band for a musical interlude during the festivities. I seconded that suggestion as it meshed perfectly with my secret plan. The introduction which I was determined to give, thankfully, went as well as I had envisioned. Prior to the talks, I tipped-off the Andy Healey that at the conclusion of my brief introduction that would like the band to play 'Danny Boy'. As I commenced my short 'roast' of the newly ordained priest, I couldn't avoid the opportunity of 'roasting' the new priest prior to my introduction. I was pleased when people commenced to laugh but I was delighted when I saw Father Dan laughing raucously to comical references of incidents in his life.

As I concluded my brief attempt at comedy I introduced... a new priest for the Archdiocese of Boston, Father Daniel Joseph Patrick Kennedy. As Father Dan proceeded to stride, with his customary gait, toward the microphone, according to plan, the band broke into a rendition of "Danny Boy," The room exploded with cheers and applause! The old man had this plan up his sleeve all along and it worked to perfection.

Yes, I thought; sometimes father does know best — and I was delighted to be rewarded with a giant hug from the new priest.

First Mass of Thanksgiving

Do not be afraid for I am with you. (Acts: 18:9b)

Father Daniel J Kennedy celebrated his First Mass of Thanksgiving m on May 27, 2007, Pentecost Sunday, at his boyhood parish, St. Joseph's Church in Needham. Father Dan offered the Mass in memory of his deceased uncle John Barrett Kennedy. Father Dan was vested in a brilliant red chasuble, a gift from his cousin, Patty Stott. He looked absolutely radiant; red vestment, red hair!

May 27th was intensely warm day, a foretaste of a hot humid summer. Prior to leaving our home for St. Joseph's he asked me to procure seven handkerchiefs for him. The house was bursting with excitement and an element of stress also permeated the air so, without questioning the specified number I followed instructions and obtained seven handkerchiefs. Father Dan was always in perpetual motion so he had a tendency to sweat excessively so I assumed, on a hot day, he was precautionary.

In retrospect I regret my reluctance to inquire as to his rationale in specifying 'seven handkerchiefs'. Father Dan never did or said anything without prior forethought; this request would undoubtedly have been well thought threw. At this point, I would undoubtedly qualify as the proverbial 'second-guesser'. Could it have been in recognition of his classmates the 'Magnificent Seven'? Could it be in tribute to the Seven Sacraments? An unanswerable question!

Many of his childhood, adolescent, and college friends were in attendance; Father Dan made it a point to remain in contact with as many friends as possible. Of course his family and his extended family participated in this joyous occasion. Father Dan's siblings proclaimed the readings, his aunts and niece Ashley presented the offertory gifts and Alice and I presented him the chalice and paten.

The Sanctuary was the locus of innumerable happy faces. The principle concelebrants comprised a few of many priests whose support was indispensable during his path to priesthood. Father

Michael Lawler, pastor of St. Joseph's (who was standing immediately at his left and discreetly coaching him during the liturgy); his old time friend Father Francis E. Reilly, with whom he visited at the Immaculate Conception Seminary in Belgium and who blessed Father Dan's chalice; (it was at Father Reilly's ordination in 1980 when Bishop Joseph F. Maguire first mentioned a vocation to young Danny); Father Charles J. Higgins, former Parochial Vicar at St. Joseph and Father Dan's longtime confidante, who also vested Dan during the Rite of Ordination was the Homilist and Father Brian Manning, his Diaconal Supervisor at St. Mary of the Nativity and a close friend was providing guidance for the Rookie Priest!

Other priests in attendance at the Mass included Father Francis M. Kennedy, who baptized Daniel Joseph on February 17, 1974; Fathers Tony Creane and David Joyce, formerly assigned to his childhood parish, St. Mary's in Westfield; and Father Jeff Statz, from the Diocese of Manchester, the close friend from seminary days whose ordination Dan attended while on leave from St. John's Seminary.

Two young seminarians served as Masters of Ceremonies, Tim Lewis and Mark Murphy. Afterward Father Dan sent them appreciative and encouraging notes and Mark told me he kept his note from Father Dan his desk at St. John's Seminary. Father Mark Murphy shared the note to Alice and me four years later on his ordination day, still grateful for Father Dan's spiritual and fraternal advice.

Father Dan blesses seminarian (and future priest) Mark Murphy.

There were numerous smiles on many happy faces as the young redheaded priest strode up and down the aisles, energetically sprinkling holy water with the strong right arm that could throw a football 40 yards. Later as he approached the most sacred portion of the Mass, the Consecration of the Precious Body and Blood of our Savior time seemed to stop as we witnessed Father Dan Kennedy consecrate the Eucharist for the first time. His eyes were rapt and his gestures deliberate in reverence for the miracle in which he was participating as he elevated the Body of Christ and lifted the Chalice of the Precious Blood. Although I was focused on the Eucharist I'm certain that moist eyes permeated the congregation with tears of joy.

After Mass, Father Dan publicly recognized some of the many people who had supported him on his journey to priesthood, with special appreciation for his sisters and brother: Katie's goodness, prayers, and advice; Patti's cheerful independence and her loving motherhood of Ashley; Anne Marie's support and loyalty "when the chips were down"; and Jack's constant, loving challenges to "up my game."

A special message of thanks went to Father Charlie Higgins for being "always ready with a kind word, a pat on the back, or, more importantly, a kick in the pants." Danny may have been coachable, but his stubborn streak never faded, and Father Charlie knew the formula for dealing with the complex redhead.

One of the Hymns Father Dan selected for his first Mass was "Christ Be Beside Me," a musical adaptation of the eighth-century Irish prayer known as St. Patrick's Breastplate. The other three — "You Are Mine," "Be Not Afraid," and "For All the Saints" — are often chosen for funerals. Indeed, when it was time to choose the music for his own Funeral Mass, I felt certain we already knew what Hymns he would prefer. I will never forget driving together, listening to his favorite CDs, when "You Are Mine," came on, he invariably shot me a grin and said, "Isn't this a great song, Dad?"

The inscription he selected for the program cover for his First Mass of Thanksgiving was entitled "Be Not Afraid" so that Hymn was also a necessity. I believed that his selection of 'For All the

Saints' was a nod to his Alma Mater, Providence College as it was reminiscent of the Providence College fight song the PC band played as he charged on to the basketball court as the Providence College Friar Mascot.

Our pastor, Father Michael Lawlor, hosted a beautiful reception after the First Mass at St. Joseph School. Father Dan later said, "My thirteen-year-old niece told me she never thought she would have to wait in line to talk with her uncle." Everyone wanted to share in such a joy filled occasion. Dozens of friends and parishioners stood in line to receive his first priestly blessing. Father Dan was delighted to see, and bless; former coaches, hockey friends from his youth along with their spouses and children, high school and college friends, and former employees from Andersen Consulting and Cabot Corporation. True friendship, like faith, survives the test of time.

That evening, two of the newly ordained priests, Father Dan and Father Matt Westcott were feted at the Knights of Columbus Hall in West Roxbury at a 'Gathering of Contemporaries'. Since their 'First Masses' were at the same time, their shared friends, many of whom traveled from out of town were forced to choose between which First Mass to attend so this was an opportunity to unite. By virtue of our dates of birth Alice and I exceeded the age limit so we were not on the invite list. This 'let your hair down' event enabled old friends of a young age, to gather once again and to rejoice with Father Dan and Father Matt. For some, it would be the first and last hurrah with Father Dan.

There was at least one, if not more, lasting benefits from the 'Gathering of Contemporaries'... our daughter Anne Marie met Dave Russell and eventually they became, Mr. and Mrs. David Francis Russell!

Fr. Dan with the future Mr. and Mrs. David Russell

After many laughs and far too many stories, Father Matt and Father Dan said their 'good-byes' so they would be able to rise early the following morning to make their 'tee time' at Mount Stratton Golf Academy in Vermont.

Chapter 12: Rookie Priest; Apprentice Parish Priest

As you sent me into the world, so I sent them into the world. (John 17:18)

Father Dan's first priestly assignment was to serve as Parochial Vicar at the beautiful and statuesque traditional redbrick St. John the Evangelist Church in Winthrop.

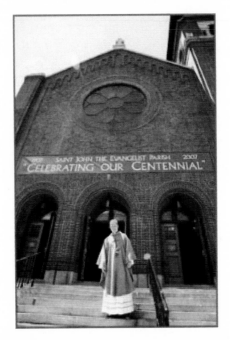

A well-maintained Colonial style Rectory, which was to be Father Dan's new home, abuts the distinctively imposing edifice. Pending completion of his room, Father Dan would be temporarily domiciled in a small room on the third floor. Father Dan was anxious to meet parishioners and eager to blend into the fabric of parish life so running up and down the three flights of stairs would count toward his daily workouts; he joked.

Father Dan's innate ebullience was matched by the enthusiasm with which the St. John parishioners welcomed him. Introducing himself at his first Mass, Father Dan said he was pleased to arrive at such a happy time for the parish, its Centennial Year; he announced his availability for any local softball team in need of a left fielder. His closing words were winsomely humble and hopeful: "Please remember that I am just a 'rookie priest' — but I will know each of you, by name, I want to be your friend and, although I am a 'rookie priest,' bear with me, I will improve!"

Between his genuine cheerfulness and his obvious enthusiasm for sharing the Good News, parishioners of all ages were taken by spirituality of this humorous, athletic priest. Many asked Father Dan directly what inspired his vocation. Oh, he had plenty of reasons, Father Dan replied, but they all boiled down to one thing, *desire*: "I wanted to do my best to ensure that, amidst our fast-paced and materialistic society, Christ remains relevant in people's everyday lives." Not an easy thing to do in today's world.

Whether in the pulpit or playing one-on-one on the basketball court, Father Dan had a coach's ability to target the message to the recipient. His classmate, Father Bob Blaney, recalled:

"Father Dan had an uncanny way of inspiring others to develop and deepen their relationship with the Lord. He accomplished this through humor — and with a real down-to-earth way of explaining matters of God and 'The Beyond.'"

In addition to integrating a new Parochial Vicar into the fabric of the parish Father Bourke supervised two seminarians during the summer months. Joseph M. Mazzone, a 4th Year Theology student from Blessed Pope John XIII National Seminary in Weston, and

Sean M. Maher, a 3rd Year Theology student from St. John's Seminary in Brighton were also in residence at St. John the Evangelist.

Acutely aware of Father Brian Manning's many kindnesses to him during his internship at St. Mary of the Nativity in Scituate, Father Dan quickly befriended both seminarians. The practicality of becoming a good priest requires much more than was is documented in a book. Joe's ordination was less than a year away so Father Dan invited him to assist with daily liturgies and frequently suggested that Joe offer a reflection at the end of Mass. Joe's confidence grew steadily, and he appreciated Dan's feedback and encouragement.

Today Father Joe Mazzone happily recalls their friendship as well as their long talks:

> *"The memories of Father Dan as a man's man are true, but not in the way that many people might think. Father Dan was a masculine guy, for sure. He was a fine athlete, he was preparing to become a Navy Chaplain, he liked a good cigar and whiskey; but in my experience Father Dan was also a real thinker. Pick a deep and profound topic, especially one involving faith, and he could talk for hours on it, a meaty and meaningful conversation."*

He saw in Father Dan a gift for empathy and receptivity:

> *"I also found him quite sensitive in the best use of that word; sensitive to the people around him, what they might be going through, the nuance and complexities of people, their emotions, and their life experiences. In other words, he was pastoral. To me, the priesthood was the perfect fit for him and his gifts."*

All of us appreciate being known as an individual, not just a face in the crowd; individuality was important to him. Father Dan adapted a corporate tactic to assist him in knowing, as an individual, every parishioner. As a by-product of his familiarity with computers, he maintained a log where he listed personal characteristics, interests, and concerns of everyone he met. It wasn't long before he was able to address each parishioner by name and provide them with feedback on whatever topic was of interest to them. His focus was always, always, on the needs of the other person.

Logan International Airport is essentially next door to Winthrop, MA. The roar of jet aircraft is incessant. Father Dan loved the location because it allowed him to do his long distant running with the Atlantic Ocean on one side of his route and the Boston skyline on the other. The 2007 Boston Marathon was the first marathon he did not run since he commenced marathon running. Consequently, he was determined to be at the starting line in Hopkinton for the 2008 Boston Marathon so it wasn't too early to begin his training regimen. Where could he possibly find a better practice route than striding around Boston Harbor?

Occasionally his schedule prevented long distance runs so he joined a local gym. When he registered the desk attendant was mystified that this redhead with white pigmentation galore adamantly refused to accept their tanning program. " Listen dude! You don't understand, dude! It's obvious, dude, you need some serious tanning! You are as white as a ghost, dude!"

As an accomplished storyteller his depiction of an event was enhanced by his ability to authentically impersonate accents and mimic dialects. Every time he told a story it was absolutely hilarious and this was no exception. It was hysterical to listen as he utilized his arsenal of skills as he dramatized the endless pressure he endured listening to the promotion of the gym's 'tanning facilities'.

As with all priests, other than celebrating Daily Mass, Father Dan's schedule was somewhat unpredictable. At any hour he might be called to a hospital, an accident or to a grieving family. This was a joy for him as he wanted to be busy and he wanted to help. In his spare time he enjoyed filling in at the Noontime Mass at St. Anthony's Franciscan Shrine in downtown Boston which also offered him the opportunity to avail himself to frequent Confession.

St. John the Evangelist Parish Ministries

Children obey your parents in the Lord for this is right, "Honor your father and mother." (Ephesians 6:1-2)

At age thirty-three, Dan had lost none of his boyishness. His sparkle and high energy served him well in his contacts with the young and the elderly of St. John the Evangelist.

One of his first encounters amounted to improvisational theater. On seeing boys playing stickball in the church's parking lot across the street, Dan charged out the door of the rectory, yelling, "Just what do you guys think you're doing playing ball on church property?" The boys knew it was not allowed and naturally were frightened to be caught red-handed. "Give me that bat," Dan ordered sternly — then grinned. "I want to take a swing." The pitcher obediently threw the ball and Father Dan blasted it across the street, banking against the side of the Rectory, to everyone's cheers.

Working with the Director of St. John the Evangelist Youth Group, Erin Flaherty, Father Dan initiated a Sunday evening Mass tailored to the youth of the parish. In order to help them better understand and participate, he explained various parts of the liturgy and soon attendance at the evening Mass for Youth increased, and, many parents attended with their children.

It wasn't long before many families began to realize that Father Dan exhibited an ability to make Christ vital in the lives of their children. Tina-Marie Talvi, Parish Cantor, said that Father Dan's energy and devotion appealed to everyone, but especially to children and teens:

> "He was ours. Our Father Dan with the brilliant smile and the quick wit. Father Dan with his unceasing ability to reach out to our kids and draw them into the love and vibrancy of Christ's world. Our Father Danny who burned so brightly with the fire of Christ's love and the need to share it."

As his niece Ashley recalled later, Father Dan was so happy in his priesthood that he seemed "luminous."

In July, Father Dan attended St. John's the Evangelist Annual Youth Outing at Canobie Lake Amusement Park in Salem, New Hampshire. He was anxious to attend even if it brought back memories of years ago when his sisters scared him into thinking we were going to abandon him at an amusement park. This time he came prepared; he drove his own car and met the group at the park. He had as much, if not more, fun as the kids.

In August there was a weeklong gathering of parish from several parishes at 'Camp Gospel Road' in central Massachusetts which was also enjoyable. The jam packed Gospel Road schedule included; spiritual discussions, sports, games, and community service in the form of painting fences. Although Father Dan appeared to be skilled in most aspects of camp activities he was definitely not 'a painter'. He had a great time; pulling pranks on anyone and everyone, swimming, and playing softball. He must have 'offered-up' his time with the paint pail as, from head to toe; he was dripping with paint! It didn't take the St. John's Youth Group long to realize his experience painting the Rectory for Father Flavin in Brockton must have been a disaster. He was so speckled with white paint he looked like a Dalmatian dog so the kids nicknamed him; "Father Drippy."

Father Dan loved to laugh, especially at himself, and was glad the young people felt comfortable enough to tease him. "Father Dan was always happy and he laughed so often because he knew God's goodness," explained his seminary pal, Father Bob Blaney.

St. John the Evangelist Religious Education Program aka Confraternity of Christian Doctrine (CCD) commences in September and extends until May. Classes are held during weekday afternoons, early evening and on Sundays. The program was well staffed with competent instructors and with a devoted staff. Father Dan was anxious to help and offered his assistance whenever needed. He realized that young people, are the future Church and they deserve solid, engaging catechesis.

The Religious Ed teachers welcomed Father Dan's involvement, including his willingness to be the disciplinarian whenever an overly enthusiastic teen needed a behavior modification. As a graduate of an all-boys high school, Father Dan knew how to handle rebellious kids.

Desire was his bye-word. It was not enough to maintain order; he wanted to instill a positive attitude, a desire to be the best. Father Dan was fair-minded and crystal clear about his expectations, constantly encouraging others to desire success and never give up on attaining aspirations. He learned well the lessons pontificated by Brother Heeran at Catholic Memorial High School.

On one occasion, a CCD instructor notified Father Dan that three students who were football players were obstreperous and classroom distractions. Father Dan called them into the office and laid down the law. He learned that the three boys ignored previous reprimands so Father Dan deemed immediate action a necessity; resultantly he informed all three that they were expelled from the CCD program. To his chagrin, all three, big muscular kids, began to cry.

Swiftly shifting gears in the face of contrition, Father Dan came up with a conditional reprieve. First, he directed, they must attend Mass every weekend. Second, they must show themselves to him or to Father Bourke after Mass. Third, they must write a weekly report on their interpretation of the Gospel and homily. The boys promptly agreed, and their expulsion was rescinded.

Several months later Father Dan ran into the same trio and stopped to ask, "How's it going?" To his delight they said they enjoyed weekend Mass and they wanted to become lectors or extraordinary ministers of the Eucharist. As Father Dan had hoped, convincing them to open their ears to God's Word at Mass was half the battle; now God was pouring His Grace into their minds and hearts.

"Father Dan loved being a priest of Jesus Christ and loved celebrating Mass," Father Joe Mazzone said. "The gift of the Eucharist was not lost on him, for sure." Father Joe remembers that Father Dan never hesitated to show his love of the Eucharist to others:

"He was distributing communion once when he saw a younger person receive it in a pretty blasé manner and

then walk back down the aisle with the Eucharist still in hand, unconsumed. Father Dan left his 'post' and followed him down the aisle and said to him, 'Do you know what that is? I've given my life for that.'

"That might strike someone as harsh, but that is not how it was received. It was a powerful witness not only to the presence of Christ in the Eucharist but also to the priesthood."

One Sunday morning when processing down the center aisle, preparatory to offer Holy Mass for the parishioners of St. John the Evangelist, he noticed a young girl holding a basketball. Father Dan always sought opportunities to communicate the Joy of Christ; instinctively he sensed this was one of those occasions. He stopped abruptly and asked sternly, "Don't you know you shouldn't bring a basketball to church?" The young girl looked abashed as he demanded; "Give me that basketball." The young girl meekly complied and handed him the basketball. Father Dan, in full view of the entire congregation, took the basketball and spun it on one finger. As the Choir continued joyfully singing the entrance Hymn the basketball seemed to spin in tune with the melody. This newly ordained, young priest, resplendent in his vestments, visibly representing Christ's Holy Priesthood, was spinning a basketball in the center aisle of St. John the Evangelist Church? After spinning the basketball for a minute he returned it to the young girl. Her frown dissipated as her smile reflected his smile and, her heart embraced the 'Joy of Christ' communicated by a joyful priest as he said; "I love basketball. Shoot well; score plenty of points." Later, that young girl, Lisa Legner, in Father Dan's honor, selected 'Daniele' as her Confirmation name.

Father Dan realized that some youngsters lack a sense of direction in their lives. He also realized that sincere praise builds confidence. He was always quick to commend achievements and to instill in them a desire to excel. One day, at the conclusion of Sunday Mass he announced that an Altar Server, John Luti, scored a "hat trick" — three goals in a single hockey game. After the congratulatory applause died down, Father Dan announced that he himself once scored a "Gordie Howe hat trick" in a hockey game: one goal; one assist; and one penalty for fighting."

Laughter has the power to unlock hearts and he certainly put a premium on unlocking hearts with laughter. The Joy of Christ abounded in his heart and he radiated that joy. As Saint Leo the Great said; *"harshness of the law might be softened by the gentleness of Grace"*.

Congeniality was one particular lesson augmented from his corporate days of behavioral training. Father Dan applied light-heartedness every day as a priest, fully convinced that every smile is a victory for God. The parish directors of Youth Ministry and Religious Education were grateful for Father Dan's efforts working with the youth of the parish. He also was actively involved in other parish ministries such as senior citizens, Home Bound parishioners, Lectors, and the Winthrop Catholic Women's Club. Although he was not an active participant (vocal ability was not amongst his gifts) he was particularly impressed with the quality of St. John's Choir.

Father Dan was delighted when he received a call from the Archdiocese of Boston soliciting his thoughts on accepting an additional responsibility; Chaplain at Blessed Pope John XXIII High School, seven miles away in Everett, MA. Father Dan always enjoyed an educational environment; immediately he accepted the proposed assignment. Duties of a high school chaplain included conducting retreats, liturgies, counseling and outreach projects. He was well suited for the assignment. While a seminarian, he had been a substitute teacher and part time hockey coach at Catholic Memorial High School so this would be an extension of those responsibilities. At Pope John XIII he would be available to influence teenagers spiritually at a critical juncture in their lives. The frosting on the cake occurred when the Principal of Pope John XXIII appointed Father Dan Assistant Hockey Coach. Have I mentioned that a true hockey player always keeps his skates handy?

Although Father Dan was not blessed with an ability to sing, he did possess a talent in winning the respect of young people. Students loved his sense of humor and pop culture references, which easily captured their attention — step one towards more serious discussion about their spiritual condition. Father Dan's personal example of enthusiasm and integrity inspired many young people to discover a genuine sense of reverence.

Richard Chisholm, Principal of Catholic Memorial School knew Father Dan as a student, as a seminarian and he knew, as a priest, Father Dan would be a positive influence on the student body so he invited him to celebrate Mass for the students at CM. Father Dan presented the Mass from the standpoint of an instructional perspective; a Teaching Mass. He explained the rubrics and elements of the liturgy in the context of the significance they have as the un-bloody Sacrifice of Christ.

Prior to celebrating Mass for the Catholic Memorial Freshmen Class, Father Dan asked the class if they knew about CM's tradition of nicknames which, once given, remain, no matter how embarrassing, for the entire four years of high school. When the freshman said they did not know of the tradition he intoned, "If anyone in attendance perceives a necessity to leave the auditorium during Mass, however valid the reason, Father Dan would ascribe a 'nickname' to the individual who would henceforth be known as — pausing a beat — Twinky! Needless to say, no one left during the Mass. Even today, the "Twinky" Mass draws smiles among the faculty at Catholic Memorial School.

Catholic Memorial High School opened their doors for the first time in September 1957 and a joyous Fiftieth Anniversary Mass was celebrated on September 8, 2007. Father Dan received an invitation to concelebrate the Anniversary Mass and to offer the Benediction at the Anniversary Dinner. Displaying the rhetorical gifts he acquired and honed at CM, Father Dan crafted a prayer of gratitude, incorporating reference to all who had been associated with Catholic Memorial High School and the Irish Christian Brothers. He recognized Blessed Edmund Ignatius Rice the founder of the Irish Christian Brothers in Waterford, Ireland, alumni, faculty, coaches, students, adjunct personnel, and even various associates who assisted in any way in perpetuating the spirit of Catholic Memorial High School. No one associated with Catholic Memorial High School was omitted from his heartfelt Benediction.

Celebrating the 50th Anniversary of Catholic Memorial High School. (L to R) Brother A. K. Cavit, CFC, Brother Anthony Bechner, CFC, MA State Rep. Michael F. Rush, Brother Dennis Gunn, CFC, and Father Dan.

Father Dan needed no "Twinky" hooks to maintain the undivided attention of the vast audience; truth and sincerity were sufficient tools of engagement.

Amongst Lifelong Friends; the Elderly

Stand up in the presence of the aged, show respect for the old, and fear your God. (Leviticus 19:32)

As the heat of the summer dissipated and the colorful leaves of autumn began to appear Father Dan settled into his newly renovated quarters in the Rectory of St. John the Evangelist Parish. At last he had sufficient space to invite Alice and I for a visit to admire his new accommodations. Bishop Robert F. Hennessey, the Auxiliary Bishop of the Central Region visited the parish on a weekend in September and Father Dan was pleased when Bishop Hennessey was complimentary on his living facilities. Father Dan was pleased to spend time with the man he had known as Father Bob, a Parochial Vicar at St. Joseph's in Needham, when he was a young boy. It was Father Bob Hennessey who first introduced him to Eucharistic Adoration at First Friday Masses at St. Joe's.

Father Dan and Bishop Bob enjoyed a fine lunch in the Town of Winthrop they had an opportunity to review his first three months as a priest. He described his duties at St. John the Evangelist and told Bishop Bob that the parishioners were most welcoming to him and he was pleased to be assigned to such a wonderful parish. After Sunday Mass, Bishop Bob told Father Dan that many parishioners thanked him for assigning such a vibrant young priest to St. John the Evangelist.

The Bishop also informed Father Dan that he needed to stop running 24/7 and make full use of his weekly day off from parish responsibilities. Use the time for recreation, such as golf or hockey, he instructed Father Dan. Blessed with this imprimatur, Father Dan decided to spend more time on the course — and treated himself to a new set of Taylor Made golf clubs.

Father Dan enjoyed life to its fullest; he loved people, he loved to play, he loved to work, and he gave himself to his priesthood full out, all in. "Being a priest doesn't mean I have a free ride into heaven," he laughed. "I must live my life in a way that's pleasing to God." Father Dan always had the big picture in mind, and even in the midst of his busy life at St. John the Evangelist he was looking ahead, thinking about where all this was going. That October on Cape Cod he mused to his sister Patti, "Imagine what it would be like to see the Face of God." Exteriorly, he was a 'happy go lucky kind of guy' but interiorly, he was a serious minded 'spiritual kind of guy'. Both aspects of his demeanor were vital components to his magnetic personality.

A young lady from the parish called to schedule an appointment for marriage instructions and Father Dan met with her and her finance in the conference room. As he was prone to do, Father Dan wanted to break the ice with an informal discussion so as to establish a relaxed and welcoming atmosphere. The young woman was from Winthrop and the young man was from Simsbury, Connecticut.

He was intrigued that the young man was from Simsbury, CT so he posed informal questions pertaining to that community. Never did he divulge that his former four-year girl friend at Providence College was from Simsbury. As he continued the friendly conversation he inquired if the young man had any hobbies or participated in any recreational sports in the Simsbury area. The young man volunteered that he was a musician and had his own band. The young man must have been inwardly perplexed as Father Dan pursued the topic of his band which culminated with the question "did your band play at a Providence College dance in 1996?"

When the young man responded in the affirmative Father Dan then inquired, "Do you remember being involved in a fight at that dance?" I can only imagine the shock on future groom's face when Father Dan pointed to himself as the other combatant and said; "that was me, I was your opponent!" Yes, in a rather unconventional way, the ice was broken and laughter ensued. Father Dan offered the bride and groom to be the option of seeking another priest for their marriage instructions but both agreed they wanted Father Dan.

Danny with his paternal grandmother on her 93rd birthday.

Since childhood Father Dan's nature was to befriend elderly people and, in his adolescent and youthful years, his interest in community service often included visiting nursing homes. In the summer of 2002, his pastoral assignment at the Jeanne Jugan Residence in Somerville, administered by the Little Sisters of the Poor, reinforced the importance of honoring and respecting older people. As a Parochial Vicar at St. John the Evangelist he was pleased to visit homebound parishioners in Winthrop. Yes, he was, 'home again'. In Father Dan's mind, home visits and other contacts with the elderly were a pleasure, never a duty, throughout his entire life, seniors always up-lifted his spirits.

Occasionally I wonder if he envied the nearness to eternity of the sick and the elderly. Perhaps his ease with them was just the natural consequence of his appreciation for their journeys. The road on which they bore their crosses was growing ever shorter; Father Dan must have seen that as cause for celebration.

Father Dan understood that nothing you say matters unless you are able to establish a rapport with people in the pews. In his homilies, Father Dan utilized his gift of humor as a rhetorical device, not simply to be a funny man but to engage the congregation. When the Boston Red Sox were in the 2007 World Series, Father Dan began his Sunday homily by announcing in a somber tone of voice, "I have a confession to make." He paused a beat to allow conjecture to enter the mind of the Mass attendees, then continuing his somber tone, he said, apologetically: "Last night I went to the World Series at Fenway Park — and I sat in box seats." After a slight pause he continued;. "For penance, I'm going again tonight, and I will sit in the bleachers!" The congregation loved his comedic delivery, which captured their attention; the prelude for his Sunday message, as he deftly tied the Scripture readings to their daily lives.

In one of their many late-night talks, Father Joe Mazzone described to Father Dan the story of a dear friend who lay dying and looked longingly at everyone in his room, as if regretting leaving them. "Dan, if you were to die, if you were in heaven," Joe asked, "do you ever think that you would want to come back?"

"No! No way! "Father Dan retorted without a moment's thought. "I wouldn't want to come back. I'd want everyone to join me!" To him the logic was perfectly obvious:

"That's where our whole lives should be headed, to be with Jesus in Heaven. That's the point of everything. It doesn't end here!"

Those words were still fresh in Joe's mind when, a few weeks later, he learned the shocking news that Father Dan died suddenly.

"Of course he's right," Father Joe wrote afterward. "The truth is that, just as Father Dan's life didn't end here, his priesthood didn't end here, either." As *a priest forever,* Father Dan "will continue to draw men to the priesthood."

Interning at St. John the Evangelist, Joe was able to observe closely as this new priest hit the ground running. He watched attentively as Father Dan taught, served, and never hid his joy in knowing that Christ loves us, unconditionally.

"Father Dan's athleticism, his masculinity, his down-to-earth qualities, even his (benign) sarcasm — which is really just teasing, a sign of affection — all of them 'hooked' people and drew them in toward Christ. I know it might be easy to romanticize all of this because of Father Dan's untimely death, but it's really true. He was a gifted man."

Father Joe became a pastor just four years after leaving the seminary, and he remains grateful today for the lessons he learned as Dan's friend and colleague at St. John the Evangelist: "Father Dan's life, and priesthood, were short, I suppose, but he lived them in a way that was fruitful, and, they will continue to be fruitful."

A Reunion, of Sorts

Blessed are the peacemakers, for they will be called children of God.
(Matthew 5:2,8)

In November 1991, Father Dan and I attended the Annual Thanksgiving Day Football Game between Catholic Memorial High School and archrival Boston College High School on the campus of Catholic Memorial in West Roxbury, MA.

It was the first time I was in a sports environment with Father Dan since his ordination and it was a thrill for me. So many people came over to speak with him; coaches, teachers, even Boston Policemen all who had formerly addressed him as 'Daniel' or 'Danny' were now addressing him as, 'Father'.

At the game, Fr. Dan's good friend from CM, Representative Mike Rush, insisted that he pose for a picture with the BC High Eagle Mascot. This brought back memories of sixteen years ago when Father Dan was the CM Silver Mascot. At a game against BC, the BC Eagle mascot ventured over to the CM sideline and initiated a confrontation with the Silver Knight. It wasn't long before the 'good nature' ribbing, in front of the CM stands, escalated and precipitated an aggressive reaction from the home team's mascot. Yes, the 'redhead' masquerading as the CM Silver Knight repelled the invading BC High Eagle who was soon to be bleeding and seeking refuge by falling at the feet of the referee on to the turf at O'Connor Field. The CM Silver Knight may have been the victorious gladiator but, subsequently, he was fearful of expulsion for a public display of fisticuffs. Fortunately, Brother Sheehan, the Principal of Catholic Memorial High School considered the incident to be in defense of the honor of Catholic Memorial High School and no punishment was adjudicated.

An interesting aside occurred at the conclusion of the game. Father Dan and I were walking toward our car when three huge CM football players verbally accosting the BC High Eagle. In a role reversal from years past, Father Dan rushed to the scene, grasped one of the players by the neck and told them to 'knock it off' and leave the Eagle alone. The intimidated football players immediately complied and, meekly, walked away. After sixteen years, the former *retaliatory* Silver Knight became a *'peacemaker'* and defended the BC High Eagle he had previously assaulted.

Chapter 13: Minister of the Sacraments

They devoted themselves to the teaching of the apostles and to the communal life, to the breaking of the bread and to the prayers. (Acts 2:42)

Whether Father Dan was celebrating Mass, hearing Confessions, Anointing the Sick, or presiding at Baptisms, Marriages, and Funerals, he tried to make each occasion an encounter with the Lord for everyone, even those people who may not be Catholic. He challenged himself to conduct every liturgical rite as a transcendent occasion of joy and hope, a transformative encounter with Christ.

"This priest standing in front of you tonight was ordained to challenge you to reach out your hand to God," he told St. John the Evangelist parishioners in a homily. "Know also that all of us will be surprised in the many places we will find Him reaching His hand out to us."

After Father Dan presided at his brother's wedding with loving humor and deep reverence, a friend wrote to Jack:

"I knew that you and Beth were going to have a memorable wedding but I have generally found Catholic weddings rather dry.... Father Dan gracefully showed that the church's traditions could be observed and honored while still properly celebrating the individuals. For me it was a tremendous ceremony; I can scarcely imagine what it must have meant to you and Beth."

*The Kennedy Family on the wedding day of John F. Kennedy
and Elizabeth B. Leonard. (L to R) Patti, Katie, Alice,
Jack, Beth, Anne Marie, Ashley, and Father Dan.*

Father Dan loved teaching the faith and preaching homilies, but to celebrate the Holy Eucharist was an indescribable thrill. In Dan's second month of priesthood he posted on Cardinal Seán O'Malley's blog a note full of joy at this glorious privilege:

> *"I am reminded of a prayer to be said before Mass which I find particularly meaningful. 'Lord may I celebrate this Eucharist in union with you, as though it were my first Eucharist, my only Eucharist, my last Eucharist.' It is my hope that I will never lose sight of the privilege it is to bring Christ, <u>truly present</u>, in the Eucharist to the good people of God."*

Every priest is challenged in many ways, not the least of which is in celebrating Holy Mass. Even the most prayerful of priests is aware of externals — the confused server, the missing vessel, late arrivals and early departures. The priest must be in tune with the congregation as he prays, on their behalf to our Almighty Father. He must also proclaim the Gospel with authenticity and deliver a well-prepared homily from the depths of a sincere heart. Most especially, the priest must also concentrate fully on the miraculous transubstantiation of bread and wine into the Body and Blood of Christ. The priest realizes that his demeanor helps to convey the sanctity of the unbloody sacrifice, but his focus must be unequivocally on the Consecration and not on himself.

As a new priest Father Dan struggled to balance these exterior and interior aspects of celebrating Mass. He often asked experienced priests whom he admired and respected how they handled distractions during the Liturgy. He was relieved when they assured him that it is normal to experience distractions. Everyone has "Martha" tendencies during "Mary" moments, they advised him. The key is to pray extensively before Mass for the Grace to devote 100% of your heart and soul to the Sacred Liturgy.

One of the priests with whom he consulted told him that God will always provide what you need; even a clumsily celebrated Mass may be an unexpected source of Grace. Father Dan was reassured by the advice of older priests, and the more he celebrated the Sacred Liturgy the more comfortable he felt. Like everything else he did in his life, determination reigned. He had an insatiable desire to celebrate Mass with a holy heart, devoid of distractions and pleasing to the Lord.

Baptisms

I prayed for this child, and the Lord granted my request. (1 Samuel 1:27)

"Happy Day of my Baptism!" On our wedding anniversary, February 17th, we could always depend on Danny calling Alice and me with that greeting followed by a raucous roar of laughter. Alice and I chose spiritually significant dates for all five baptisms: September 8th, the birthday of the Blessed Mother; January 6th, the Feast of the Epiphany; and in Danny's case our anniversary date. It was our hope that associating the date of an event with their baptism would assist them in recalling the date they were welcomed into the Catholic Church. I am not certain that our family plan was effective with all of our kids but in Danny's case it certainly was effective. Every year he recalled with joy, the date of his baptism into the church of his friend, Jesus Christ.

Alice and I were delighted when Patti maintained our family tradition and arranged to have her daughter, Ashley, baptized on March 13th, my father's birth date.

As a deacon, Dan was permitted to baptize at St. Mary of the Nativity during his last months as a seminarian. He considered it an honor to be asked to officiate at a baptism. In his mind, Baptism enjoyed precedence on any scheduling conflict; he willingly rearranged his schedule to accommodate the parent's request. He truly treasured every opportunity to welcome a baby, or an adult, into the Catholic Church. Father Dan's last ministerial act, on the day he died, was baptizing Kelly Elizabeth Blute in Fairfield, CT, the daughter of Matt and Erin Blute.

One day when Father Dan was at a local 'gym' he received an urgent call informing him that a priest was needed at a Boston Hospital where a two-year-old boy lay dying after swallowing a marble. When Father Dan arrived at the hospital he was furious to learn that the child had never been baptized, the young boy's mother was in absentia and the boy had been in the care of his father when the accidental swallowing of marble occurred. In spite of the father's spiritual irresponsibility Father Dan spoke gently and lovingly to the distraught man and convinced him to consent to allow him to baptize the 2 year old. As Father Dan proceeded to unpack his kit of oils and holy water, he began to quietly explain the purpose and power of all aspects of Baptism and the Sacrament of Anointing the Sick. The girlfriend of the boy's father was also in the room. Both of them watched and listened intently as Father Dan reverently baptized the dying child. Afterward he prayed with the young couple, keeping watch as the child entered eternal life. Father Dan was deeply impacted by this incident; deeply disturbed that the young boy had died but grateful that he died a baptized Catholic.

The story did not end there, however. Father Dan did not know that the girlfriend was pregnant at the time and planning to have an abortion, but his gentle words about God's love lingered in her heart and, she changed her mind and did not have an abortion. When Father Dan learned of this later, he marveled at the magnitude of God's goodness. From a terrible tragedy; salvation for one baby and life for another!

Matrimony

The Lord God said: It is not good for the man to be alone. (Genesis 2:18a)

When he was a third-year theology student, Dan went to Maine to give a reflection at his cousin Meaghan Masi's marriage, and his listeners were impressed with his spiritual insight. Once he became Deacon Dan he had the authority to officiate at weddings, and in May 2007, at the request of his good friends Billy Condron and Julie Fogarty he went to St. Louis, Missouri to officiate at their wedding. His homily reminded them of their spiritual roots:

"Julie and Billy, you are the product of wonderful parents, people of faith. We truly believe that God has spoken to you in many, many ways and the virtues instilled in you by your parents have brought you together.... Two thousand years ago Christ elevated the natural union of man and woman to a sacramental level. Sacraments confer grace, and sacramental grace is essential in a joyful, happy, healthy marriage."

Then he spoke to each of them, first the bride:

"Julie, you have chosen the month of May in which to be married. This month is known as the month of Mary, the Mother of Christ. Always imitate the virtues of Mary, the Mother of our Lord."

Then the groom:

"Billy, this past week the church has observed the Feast of St. Joseph the Worker, the guardian of Christ. During your married life, always imitate the virtues of St. Joseph. Let him be your beacon."

The Holy Family was the perfect image to depict, for they bore troubles together in faith and rejoiced to follow the will of God.

On October 13, 2007, Father Dan witnessed his brother Jack's marriage to Beth Leonard. Father Dan was his usual affable self, smoothly blending reverent spirituality with humorous, human touches. Beth's uncle, Tom Dunn, was impressed with the way Father Dan conducted the wedding ceremony, and the next day he presented Father Dan with a Chalice which belonged to his uncle, who died twelve years earlier. Tom said ; "For twelve years I haven't known what to do with the chalice but after witnessing the way Father Kennedy celebrated the Sacrament of Matrimony yesterday I want to pass the Chalice on to 'another good priest'."

When I learned that the owner of the chalice had been Father James "Wicky" Sears, I knew I had an interesting story to tell Dan linking our family to 'Wicky' Sears. It goes like this...

I had never known my uncle Maurice "Mossy" Kennedy, who had died at age 17 from injuries sustained in a Cathedral High School basketball game. Mossy was an excellent student and an outstanding high school athlete whose lifelong ambition was to become a priest. After Mossy died, his closest friend resolved to enter the seminary in his place. As a young boy I met that priest, who told me, "I entered the seminary because my best friend, your uncle, died; I took his place." That priest was Father 'Wicky' Sears.

Father Sears' chalice, graciously presented to Father Kennedy, has since been inscribed; Father James P. Sears, Ordained May 22, 1937 presented to Father Daniel J. Kennedy, Ordained May 26, 2007. The Chalice is currently used at Daily Mass in St. Joseph's Church in Needham.

Another October wedding was held on the 27th of the month. Father Dan officiated for the wedding of State Representative — now State Senator — Mike Rush and Mary Foster. Father Dan and Mike had been pals since freshman year at Catholic Memorial, and Mike tapped Dan to run his successful campaigns for class president there and at Providence College.

Father Dan's homily had plenty of inside information, but his kidding, as always, turned into a spiritual lesson. "Mary was put here on this earth to help you, Mike, into heaven, "Father Dan told his longtime friend Mike. To Mary, the bride he said, "Mike was put on this earth to help you, Mary, into heaven." Then he loudly ordered them both, "Make certain you fulfill this assignment!"

November brought another wedding, this time for two more of his close friends, Patrick Murphy and Christina Carrion. Although Father Dan never met Patrick's late and well-loved father, in his homily Father Dan, paraphrasing John 14;7, announced:

"I knew Mr. Murphy. Mr. Murphy was kind, thoughtful, and a prayerful man. He was a caring father, a faithful husband, a wonderful human being, and he played a fine game of golf. The reason I knew Mr. Murphy is because I know his son, Patrick; 'if you know the Son, you know the Father.'"

Father Dan concluded by reminding the couple of their spiritual responsibilities: to constantly help each other toward heaven. "When there are disagreements or challenges," he advised, "think: Let the greater one be me." He paused, and then underscored his message: "Write it down. Knit it on an afghan. Remember it!"

Confession

Repent, therefore, and be converted, that your sins may be wiped away. (Acts 3:19)

Father Dan treasured the Sacrament of Reconciliation and he felt deeply every confessor had a duty to put the penitent at ease, be welcoming, listen intently and to truly portray the embodiment of forgiveness for every penitent and to always counsel penitents as he himself would like to be counseled. He realized that everyone, including the confessor, is a sinner so there was no room for confessor arrogance regardless of the severity of the sin. Father Dan was very much in awe of the power of Confession thus, like everything he did, the desire to do it well was paramount and the desire to put people at ease and to; 'be not afraid' mandatory.

Father Bill Lohan remembers well Father Dan's deep respect for the Sacrament of Reconciliation. "When we were out socially, if 'Dissatisfaction with Confession' ever came up during a discussion he would immediately suggest that the dissatisfied person, give it another chance. He would also recommend good and holy priests and assure the person that they would be blessed with a worthwhile experience."

Early in his priesthood Father Dan encountered an interesting reaction from a youngster in a 'face to face' confessional. When Father Dan raised his hand to give absolution, the youngster slapped him a high-five. "I have a vivid remembrance of Father Dan telling me that story; he was laughing so hard at the incredible human reaction of sacramental relief," Father Bill recalls. "On other occasions it has also happened to me, of course I think of him right away."

One day I mentioned to Father Dan my reaction to the Sacrament of Reconciliation. I told him that I realize I the power of absolution but I also feel a sense of exhilaration; an increase in self-confidence and strength. He concurred, and assured me that the Sacrament of Reconciliation is so powerful that its grace continues long after we leave the confessional box.

Father Dan illustrated that point unknowingly. After he passed away a friend of mine from St. Anthony's Shrine on Arch Street in downtown Boston related to me an interesting story. Prior to officially commencing his assignment at St. Brigid's Church in South Boston the pastor asked him to assist at the parish's First Confession for youngsters. A woman who had not been to church in many years, attended the First Confession to support her niece. As the children sat nervously in their pews, a young redheaded priest strolled into the Sanctuary then pulled up short, staring at a strip of colored tile on the floor of the Sanctuary. Pointing to strip, he asked the children, "What is this, the foul line at the Boston Garden?"

Giggles ensued; anxiety abated; the woman's niece was one of many kids who changed pews to be near that priest's Confessional Station. Afterward the excited little girl told her aunt how thrilled she was to go to Confession to such a kind young priest; on the spot she decided to go to that young priest when it was the adults' turn. It was of course, Father Dan and he heard her Confession just a few days before his death. After so many years away from the Sacrament of Reconciliation, a little girl's excitement precipitated her aunt's return to the sacraments.

Evangelization

Behold, I am sending you like sheep in the midst of wolves; so be shrewd as serpents and simple as doves. (Matthew 10:16)

Father Dan was continually seeking opportunities to evangelize. What better terrain to till than the fertile soil of Christmas or Easter when churches are packed with unimaginably tremendous numbers of people? He was determined to devote a considerable portion of his priesthood to convincing people to attend Mass more frequently than once or twice a year.

Occasionally, Father Dan posed challenges in his homilies realizing that while people respond to a pat on the back, at times, a challenge or a kick on the posterior may also be effective. On Christmas Eve he challenged people to meditate on the Incarnation; our needs for guidance, and the endless distractions that draw us away from God. He continued: "My challenge for all those gathered here at St. John the Evangelist on this most Holy Night is to *step up your game*. Step it up in the name of the Lord, and make no apologies."

With a nod to the recently concluded election and the political ads relentlessly permeating our television sets, Father Dan closed: "My name is Father Dan Kennedy, and I approve this message, in the name of the Father, and of the Son, and of the Holy Spirit." Father Dan always ended his homilies with one of his most cherished sources of spiritual support; the sign of the cross; trusting in God to mend any flaws in the content or in the delivery of his message.

Without a doubt he recognized that the Sacrament of Matrimony was fertile ground for evangelization. He was honored to officiate at marriages and was hopeful of receiving an invitation to the Wedding Reception of the bride and groom. We didn't disagree often but this was one of those issues on which we did not agree. I pointed out the perceived impropriety of a young priest partaking in wedding festivities which may become overt social extremes. I pointed out that with the drinking and dancing and sometimes racy outfits on women. He pointed out that he was in the world not of the world and that his years of 'worldly exposure' qualified him to successfully deal with people on their own terrain. I knew he could lead a conga line with the best of them; what if he somehow forgot he was now a "black suit," not a "corporate suit"?

Father Dan disagreed and proceeded to lecture me on the opportunity to harvest many souls that don't realize they are longing for a relationship with Christ. First, he pointed out that a wedding draws young people who otherwise might not regularly attend Mass, so, to him; it is an ideal opportunity to connect with disaffected or indifferent people. Secondly, a priest looks more approachable amid the revelry of a party atmosphere — especially after someone has had a few drinks. Thirdly, he loved it when strangers started dumping their complaints and criticisms about the Church on him. This played right into his master plan.

His method in dealing with what would appear to be an obstreperous person was to put a big smile on his face and say warmly, "You've come to the right person with that observation! I'm currently writing a paper about that topic, so I will definitely be able to discuss that matter with you." He knew that letting them vent would bring them around to a more open frame of mind. At that point, still smiling, he could utilize his knowledge on the subject to present a powerful and persuasive explanation often dispelling the concerns of an agitated wedding guest.

Father Dan's friendliness invariably disarmed people, and slowly but surely Father Dan would guide them so eventually they would admit that spiritual truths matter — and to realize that the state of their soul mattered to him. He had infinite patience and infinite guile, following the advice to be *"shrewd as serpents and simple as doves."* (Matthew 10:16b).

Even his young niece Ashley could see how well Uncle Dan worked crowds. "He was the best," she recalled. "He was able to change the notions people had about the Catholic Church." Wherever he went, "he had an ability to reel in a wide variety of people of all ages, races, professions, with varying interests — people that had strayed away from the church, or weren't necessarily religious, and he was able to captivate them."

Ashley said his secret was simply to treat everyone with full respect as a child of God, helping them feel how deeply we all yearn for spiritual meaning. "When you stumble upon someone who truly strikes you, penetrates the surface of your subconscious and makes you think or challenge what you previously accepted, that feeling lingers," Ashley observed. "You may walk away, but that influence remains with you."

Father Dan took seriously the state of a stranger's soul, but he did it in a lighthearted, engaging fashion. Ashley said his passions were God, practicing his faith and sharing that faith. This "luminous" man "had an ability to knock on the doors people forgot they had."

His sister Katie had similar tales from her visits with Dan the Man and subsequently, Father Dan. Katie said that he was particularly pleased to wear the Roman Collar as it served as a magnet to bring aggrieved people to him. Wherever he was, at weddings, funerals, tailgate parties, sooner or later someone would disparage the Church, or the clergy, or the pope. Father Dan was always delighted in seizing that moment he did not come unarmed he came fully prepared for dialogue. Open mouths gave way to open ears and, gradually, open ears gave way to open hearts. Father Dan's skillful prodding disarmed the agitated and he countered with knowledge, genuine concern, love, and conviction; all presented with an unfailing and uplifting sense of humor.

I admit I was skeptical of Father Dan's approach, but now I know he was right. At his wake several young people approached me to say that because of meeting Father Dan at a wedding they had returned to the Church. I was reminded that after presiding at a wedding his last words were often simple and direct: "Go to Mass!"

Funeral Masses

Blessed are they who mourn, for they will be comforted. (Matthew 5:4)

As a boy serving at Funeral Masses, Danny had many opportunities to ponder the concept of a soul in transit to eternal life. He saw the grief and tears of the mourners, of course, but he also heard the words of hope and promise in the liturgy. As a priest Father Dan offered Funeral Masses at St. John the Evangelist and, as with baptisms and weddings, he felt honored when anyone requested that he preside.

Shortly after he arrived at St. John the Evangelist he was asked to visit a Boston Hospital to anoint a dying woman. As he sat at her bedside the woman asked him if he knew what Heaven was like. He was momentarily taken aback by the forthright question, but without hesitation he quickly responded; "No, I don't know what Heaven is like but, in two days you're going to know what Heaven is like and the rest of us will still be down here scratching our heads". His response might appear brash or insensitive but it was characteristically, Father Dan. With a direct, unencumbered, and, to the point response, he communicated love and hope. Often, he spoke with a bit of inherited Irish wit; always, he spoke from the heart and, with love.

After Father Dan left the hospital the woman told her daughter that she would like that young priest to celebrate her Funeral Mass at St. John the Evangelist. Two days later the Parish Administrator received a request that Father Kennedy celebrate her Funeral Mass. The parish staff kidded him when they said; "You have only been here for two days and already we are receiving requests for you to celebrate Mass".

That summer of 2007 Father Dan was invited to celebrate and concelebrate funeral Masses for close friends, including his former pastor at St. Joseph's, Father Jim Haddad. He considered it an honor and a blessing to participate at the Holy Sacrifice of the Mass for the dearly departed. It was particularly significant to the bereaved family when the celebrant was blessed to have known the deceased and could speak personally about their lives and their gifts — a consoling familiarity that every mourner appreciates.

Father Dan knew that touching his listeners' hearts would help them trust in the truth proclaimed at each Funeral Mass: Christ's irrevocable promise of salvation. We may fail Him, but He never fails us.

Chapter 14: Advent at Sea, Christmas at Home

We saw his star at its rising and have come to do him homage. (Matthew 2:2)

During the first two weeks of December 2007, Lieutenant Dan Kennedy was on active duty as a Chaplain with the United States Navy, deployed on a nuclear-powered aircraft carrier, the USS Nimitz, CVN-68 traversing the Pacific Ocean. The 'Nimitz' was carrying "its full complement of sailors, pilots, and Marines, five thousand aboard," Dan wrote to me in an email.

"I am really learning to know the ship. We are receiving in-depth tours of all major departments. What an operation. We have been experiencing high seas. You wouldn't believe how much the deck of such a huge ship heaves in the waves. As you can imagine that affects life all over the ship. The treadmill at night becomes a whole new ball game."

He was impressed by the constant activity. "These guys work hard on this ship. The enlisted guys — and officers, too — pull 15–18 hour days, every day."

After a few days on the Nimitz he was flown by helicopter to a support vessel, the USS Princeton, CG-59 to hear confessions, and celebrate Mass. I assumed that my tough athlete would think nothing of a chopper trip over choppy seas from one ship to another, but in an email he wrote, "Dad, I was petrified, but I had my Chalice with me so I was all set." The way the waves ceaselessly tossed the cruiser Princeton tested Father Dan's sea legs — and brought home the power of nature and the smallness of man.

Everything was a new experience:

"The stars out here are unlike anything I have ever seen; they are absolutely brilliant; so bright and so many of them. So far the roll of this ship has not bothered me. The crew all seemed to think the roll would make me sick; so far so good. Sleeping will be a challenge, though. I did end up with a glass of water in my lap at lunch, while eating with the Captain of the ship."

Father Dan was struck by the youth of the crew — "This shop seems to be run by young guys and gals, whereas those in control of the carrier were all in their 40s and 50s." He was also amused by how many heard his accent and came up to introduce themselves as fellow natives of Massachusetts.

The Holy Sacrifice of the Mass drew a large turnout, and the eagerness for the Eucharist was humbling for Father Dan: "They were so happy just to be present at Mass. When sailors have been deprived of the Mass, the priest really just needs to stay out of the way and let them be drawn into the Eucharist, as opposed to doing cartwheels during the homily (at least that's the way I think)."

In a homily, Lieutenant (Father) Kennedy directly addressed the perceived societal pressure of self-sufficiency confronting young men and young women in today's world which culminates in abandonment of the Church. For five years he knew, firsthand, daily pressure to work hard, play hard, and to live in the fast lane and to do it all on your own terms:

"I hear it all the time, from friends and family members: "Church doesn't work for me; why do we have go? Rules don't work for me; nobody should tell me how to worship". To them I say: Tell me about the last time 'secular society' led you to re-engage the mystery of God's love for us. We need the Church. It is through the Church and through the sacraments that Jesus has chosen to remain with us."

"...My own brand of spirituality — I'm spiritual; not religious — isn't all that matters, just being a good person? If you are truly that confident in yourself and your ability to navigate the waters of this life, and in your ability to stay afloat despite the waves of uncertainty and struggle in this life, and in your own ability to reach the shore on the other side, then I wish you 'fair winds and following seas'."

"But St. Paul reminds us this week that it is in our recognition of our poverty, our own weakness, that we find our

strength. As we recognize our dependence upon God, we are given the strength and the motivation to return His love to him through worship and, in turn, to share that love with our neighbor through action. This is the meaning of Advent; "prepare the way of the Lord."

As usual, Lieutenant Kennedy concluded his homily with the Sign of the Cross.

"In the name of the Father, and of the Son, and of the Holy Spirit. Amen."

At another Mass, Lieutenant Kennedy challenged his shipmates to "strive for sainthood," and he was pleased to find that the challenge resonated well. No one in the service wants to settle for second best, and Lieutenant Kennedy struck the right chord when he urged them to keep striving to know and serve God. His homily reflected his focus on practical realities:

"We can talk and talk about God and spirituality, but it is the doing where we need to focus. If you are a nice person, try becoming a really nice person. Strive for sainthood. Nobody talks about that anymore. It may seem too lofty or too idealistic, or you may be thinking, "Get a clue, Father." Actually, the more we hear these things, the less bizarre they sound."

"So much of our tradition requires faith; we need to continue to stoke the fires of faith in our hearts and our minds. Christ is truly present in the Sacraments, none more so than the Eucharist. He has provided us with these real sacramental encounters with Him so that we might achieve sainthood."

"...It is our job to encourage society to worship God. We encourage by our actions, by how we live out our daily lives. Is there something different about the way we carry ourselves as a result of our practice of our faith? Well, there should be. It is our actions which speak the loudest. When our actions are good and charitable, then there is absolutely no need to push our own brand of spirituality on others; they will follow, or at least be intrigued by, our example."

"Drop in on that neighbor you think of every once in a while. Wave someone ahead in traffic — not just once, but as a rule. Volunteer at that soup kitchen or homeless shelter and, perhaps most challenging of all, summon more patience for someone who frustrates you. Some of these actions might be difficult at first, but they are steps along the path to sainthood. With each action we are converting our hearts and minds toward Christ."

After his sojourn on the high seas Lieutenant Kennedy returned to Winthrop shortly before Christmas. He presumed that he would be celebrating a Christmas Day Mass but he was wrong. Father Bourke assigned him to celebrate the 6:00pm Mass on Christmas Eve, which historically, was less well attended than other Christmas Masses. Father Bourke rationalized that Mass would be less intimidating for a new priest.

Every Christian loves Christmas but Danny had always exhibited an intense love the 'Birthday of the Lord' and it was his aspiration to celebrate Mass on Christmas Day. In his mind, Advent prepared us for Christmas Day. In days past December 24th was meatless and the Christmas celebration commenced at Midnight on December 25th. As a young boy, even at Alice's behest to open one present on Christmas Eve he refused. Regardless of the rest of the family he only opened his presents on Christmas Day. When Father Dan told me he felt disappointed that his first Christmas Mass would be the vigil, not the day itself, I pointed out that it was a small sacrifice for the privilege of bringing people the gift of the Eucharist on the Vigil of Christmas Day. He had to agree.

"Some Christmas Eve Masses can be "a crazy zoo," recalls Tina-Marie Talvi, the Cantor at St. John the Evangelist remarked. Shortly before the 4:00 p.m. Mass which traditionally is jam packed, she witnessed Father Dan's amazement as the pews filled with a buzzing throng, yet he seemed relaxed and well composed. "Do you think I have time to write my homily for the 6:00 p.m. Mass?" he joked, Tina-Marie laughed at his attempt at light-heartedness.

Of course, his two proud parents were in attendance at his first Christmas Eve Mass anxiously waiting for the entrance hymn; 'O Come All Ye Faithful' to commence. Much like the pleasant surprise we experienced on the seventh of April 2007, when he processed down the aisle of St Mary of the Nativity at the Easter Vigil chanting the Exultet. Our hearts began to beat faster on the twenty fourth of December 2007 (24/7) as he joyously processed down the center aisle of St. John the Evangelist Church, resplendent in a brilliant golden chasuble. His beaming smile unequivocally communicated the merriment in his heart as he prepared to celebrate Christmas Eve Mass.

Father Dan offered a powerful homily comparing the brightness of the stars he observed over the Pacific Ocean when he was, most recently, deployed on the USS Nimitz with *The Star of Bethlehem*.

Father Dan pointed out that the brilliance of the stars was even more prominent in the context of the silence of the night and the blackness of the sea. He drew a similarity between the stars over the Pacific in December of 2007 with what must have been the silence of the night and the brightness of The Star on the First Christmas in Bethlehem. He pointed out that; "2000 years ago there were no neon signs, no street lights, no city sounds, and no electronic tracking devices; just the brilliance of *The Star of Bethlehem* shinning over the Manger. On that Holy Night, in the silence of a stable, God gave mankind a Gift of Love which brought *Everlasting Light* to a darkened World."

Father Dan related an incident that occurred on board the Nimitz to the transfixed parishioners at St. John the Evangelist. He explained that one night when he was on the flight deck viewing the beauty of the stars a sailor, who was on night watch, approached and began to discuss the impressive stars. The sailor, equally enthralled with the magnificence of the millions of stars in the galaxy said to him; 'I wish my mother could be here to share the beauty of these stars'.

He went on to say:

"That sailor's urge to share the beauty of the stars with someone he loved was — just like all of us who share "Christmas Carols, presents, greetings, get-togethers with those we love which is our version of the Christmas Story. Just as God the Father shared His Son and His Love, with the whole world on that First Christmas so also do we share with others our love on this and every Christmas."

"I cannot begin to tell you how heartwarming it is for this rookie priest to see this church so crowded, so full of joy, excitement, anticipation," Father Dan said, reminding everyone why they were gathered. "It fills me with great hope that, despite all that Christ's Church has been through these past several years, Christ's Love is so powerful that we still

*feel the need to share it, to celebrate it, to give thanks for
it and, for all that is good in our lives."*

As he had done for the crew and officers at sea, Father Dan
then offered a list of practical how-tos:

*"Love others as you love yourself. Lay down what is import-
ant to you, in favor of what is important to others. Be extra
patient with those we find frustrating. Love the Lord your
God with all your heart, with your entire mind and with all
your soul. Tell the truth. Be charitable in word and action.
Place nothing before the Lord your God. Keep holy the
Sabbath."*

Father Dan realized that at Christmas Masses the congregation
would welcome both faithful parishioners and also lapsed Catholics and believers who had been alienated by the recent abuse
scandal. He could have ignored the topic. Instead he disarmed his
listeners by pointing out that the failure of others is no excuse for
abdicating our own responsibilities. We do have spiritual responsibilities; in particular, we have the duty, as well as the privilege, to
attend Sunday Mass, where God strengthens us for the daily trials
of life.

*"Let me say it again, it is so great to see so many faithful
in attendance tonight. At the 4:00 p.m. Mass they were
standing in the aisles, and there are hardly any empty seats
here tonight. Oh, what a problem to have! My prayer is
that our Church will once again become 'full to capacity' so
that many more people may experience the joy of active
participation in our Church."*

"Our society combined with many responsibilities in life discourages the regular worship of our God. My challenge for all those gathered at St. John the Evangelist on this most holy night is to step up your game, step it up in the name of the Lord, and make no apologies."

"I am proud to be a member of our Catholic Church, especially when it is on the upswing! Take a look around, be encouraged by the show of force we see here tonight. Take this joy, so visible tonight, and carry it with you throughout the year. Revisit this joy in your heart, apply it in your actions, and revisit the joy of the Lord around His Altar, where He is truly present in the most Holy Sacrifice of the Mass."

Always one to "leave 'em laughing," Father Dan closed by referencing the past autumn's election season when, on a daily basis, political television advertisements, ended with the candidate identifying him or herself culminating with their affirmation of the message.

"May the joy and peace of the Christ Child be yours today and forever."

"My name is Father Dan Kennedy, and I approve this message."

Followed by his signature Sign of the Cross, 'sign off':

"In the Name of the Father, and of the Son, and of the Holy Spirit. Amen."

As Alice and I left the church, the expression on every face radiated with Christmas Joy; the Light of Christ.

On Christmas Day, after all Masses had concluded, Father Dan parked his car in his usual spot in front of our home for our family Christmas Celebration. As was his custom, before exiting his car he paused for a few seconds, pretending to adjust his rear view mirror, to make the Sign of the Cross on his forehead and say a quick prayer.

We ate, drank, and were merry; it was a happy time together, and to this day I treasure my 2007 Christmas Present. It was a Mass card inscribed;

"The Holy Sacrifice of the Mass will be offered for the intentions of Daniel J. Kennedy, Sr., by Reverend Daniel J. Kennedy" and signed: "Danny, Katie, Patti, Anne Marie, and Jackie."

"It doesn't get much better than this," I muttered with a choking voice and moist filled eyes, as Alice gave Danny and me big hugs. Actions speak louder than words.

Chapter 15: Same Skyline; Different Angle

For your name's sake lead me and guide me. (Psalm 31:4)

As happy as he was at St. John the Evangelist, Father Dan felt underutilized on weekends. During the week he was busy with homebound visits, religious education responsibilities, daily Mass, and duties at Pope John XXIII High School in Everett. He was a dynamo and felt fulfilled when expending his abundant energy.

Weekend Mass assignments were distributed amongst Father Charlie, Father Dan, visiting priests and retired priests. One of the retired priests sensed Father Dan's eagerness to celebrate Mass as often as possible and offered to share his assignments, but Father Dan declined. The gift of offering Mass is a joy for every priest and Father Dan would not deprive a man, who gave his life to Christ's priesthood, the privilege of celebrating a Sunday Mass.

Surprisingly, an opportunity presented itself which would enable him to expend his pent-up weekend energy. Two parishes in South Boston, Gate of Heaven and St. Brigid, which included a school, were recently linked together creating an opening for a Parochial Vicar. Father Dan prayed and deliberated for several days before he decided to apply for the Parochial Vicar opening. Father Dan was hesitant to submit an application for fear he would unduly upset the parishioners he had come to truly love at St. John the Evangelist. It disturbed Father Dan that parishioners might be disappointed if he were to be transferred after only eight months at

St. John the Evangelist; he knew they had deep affection for their 'rookie priest'. However, the need for a high-octane parochial vicar in Southie combined with Father Dan's desire to celebrate week-end Masses at two parishes and, with a parish school to boot were powerful incentives. With his youth, health and unbridled energy, Father Dan hoped that the archdiocese would concur that he was a strong fit for a multiple parish assignment.

Gate of Heaven and St. Brigid

This is nothing else but the house of God, the gateway to heaven! (Genesis 28:17)

Within a few weeks the archdiocese informed Father Dan that his transfer had been approved and would become effective on the last Tuesday of the month, January 29, 2008. Soon afterwards, dining at a South Boston restaurant with a few friends Father Dan overheard a few women speculating on who would be the new Parochial Vicar at Gate of Heaven and St. Brigid. Father Dan couldn't help but hear their speculation; immediately, he ventured over to their table and, radiating his customary enthusiastic smile, he introduced himself as the new Parochial Vicar.

In a sense he was being somewhat presumptuous, for his appointment had not as yet been publicized. The women were most welcoming and they were delighted to be the first parishioners to meet the new Parochial Vicar. One of the women remarked that the entire parish would be delighted to welcome a redheaded priest to 'Southie'. He may have been unduly forthright in pre-empting the official announcement but their enthusiasm affirmed his initial instinct; don't hold back when you are representing the Lord! Don't keep His Light under a bushel basket; let it shine, let it shine! Vintage Father Dan Kennedy. Even though he hadn't officially been assigned to Gate of Heaven/St. Brigid, Father Dan felt he was off to a good start.

He was so excited when he told Alice and me that he could not wait to show us Gate of Heaven as it is "the most beautiful church in the Archdiocese of Boston!" Gate of Heaven, with a beautiful nave, soaring columns, and distinctive altar, and gorgeous stained-glassed windows had been a place where thousands of Irish immigrants received the sacraments. Of course he also wanted us to see St. Brigid, the church Katie attended when she lived in South Boston a few years earlier, where he intended to celebrate Mass on February 3, 2008.

Father Dan anticipated a smooth acclimation to parish life in South Boston. He knew many people from his hockey days and from the annual St. Patrick's Day Parade. His customary enthusiasm and self-confidence was in evidence for all to see. He considered the Southie assignment as a 'homecoming' of sorts. Father Dan was also looking forward to a new route to run in his ongoing training program for the 2008 Boston Marathon. South Boston is on the southerly side of Boston Harbor so he would still have a comparable view as did he in Winthrop. He would also hear the same jet air traffic he became accustomed to hearing as he ran his daily route on the Winthrop shoreline. Logan International Airport is sandwiched between both communities so in a sense he was still 'at home'. Marathon training would still provide a view of Boston Harbor just from a different perspective. He was looking forward to running past Castle Island, Carson Beach, the statue of Father Joseph Laporte (a South Boston priest who was so loved in Southie), with the President John F Kennedy Memorial Library at Columbia Point in Dorchester in the background and finally, the University of Massachusetts where he first played hockey in Eastern Mass as a seven-year-old Needham Mite.

A few days before Father Dan's official start at Gate of Heaven/ St Brigid's, Father Robert Casey, the pastor, invited him to hear the second grade kid's First Confession, with dinner at the rectory beforehand. Father Dan ducked into the kitchen afterward to compliment the cook. "That meal was wonderful," he praised her. "You and I are going to become good friends!"

Every athlete burns off calories, and Father Dan's formidable appetite, complimented his exceedingly high rate of energy and kept his metabolism percolating efficiently. With his insatiable appetite he certainly appreciated practitioners of the culinary arts, as he broadened his taste buds in Paris, Sao Paulo, San Francisco, and Manhattan. Even though he did enjoy 'fine dining' Father Dan loved home cooking and that appeared to be an ancillary benefit of serving at Gate of Heaven/St. Brigid's Parishes.

With the prospect of a busy schedule, two parishes and one school, he was anxious to 'roll up his sleeves'. Father Dan was certain his future in South Boston would be of benefit to the parish and he couldn't wait to begin and, he couldn't wait for us to join him at Sunday Mass on February 3rd.

A Time to Weep...

(Ecclesiastes 3:4)

As his tenure in Winthrop was winding down, Father Dan spent a few days with us in Needham. On Thursday evening, January 24, 2008, he offered his daily Mass on the marble tabletop in our living room for the repose of the soul of Alice's recently deceased cousin, Bob Stierle, and he asked Alice to proclaim the Readings. Although we did not realize it, this would be the last time Alice and I witnessed him celebrating Mass.

As I learned later, Father Dan asked our pastor, Father Michael Lawlor, for permission to offer his daily Mass on Friday, January 25th in St. Joseph's downstairs chapel. In view of the fact that, on Fridays, St. Joseph's reserves the downstairs church for Eucharistic Adoration Father Lawlor suggested that he offer Mass at the main altar in the upstairs church. Coincidentally, I happened to drive past St. Joe's on Friday morning so I decided to drop in at Eucharistic Adoration. As I was entering the side door, I met Father Armano as he was exiting. We greeted each other as we passed but did not engage in conversation. Father Armano presumed I was going to the upstairs church to witness Father Dan's Mass; I was not.

In fact, neither Father Dan nor I knew the other was in the same edifice — and neither of us could have imagined that this would be Father Dan's final Mass in Needham. Quite an interesting scenario: Father Dan celebrating a Private Mass with only his friend Jesus in attendance, at the Altar of his youth, the same Altar where he celebrated his First Mass of Thanksgiving on May 27th, Pentecost Sunday, just a short eight months ago. On the octave of his First Mass, almost to the day, he offered his final Mass on January 25th; he would die two days later on January 27th precisely a year to the day of his ordination to the diaconate.

Alice was thrilled when Father Dan devoted the rest of the day to cleaning out his bedroom and his corner of our garage, where his belongings had been piling up for over a decade. Although neither Alice nor I had any idea of what prompted him to embark on that project we were pleased. As Alice drily observed; "There is a first time for everything."

As usual, I was drafted to participate in the disembarking process. After Father Dan filled the back porch with overflowing cardboard boxes and numerous Needham Yellow Bags designated, 'Transfer Station' he asked me to transport them to the Needham Transfer Station (aka Needham Dump). As I was about to toss various items into designated bins I was surprised to see the extent of the purging process: picture albums, trophies, yearbooks — even what looked to me like perfectly good clothes. After culling a few items I deemed worth of preserving I headed back home, pleased to have helped our priest son to clear out his debris. Upon arrival home, I discovered that a domestic catastrophe had erupted.

In clearing the porch I, inadvertently, confiscated some Raggedy Ann dolls dating from Katie's earliest years. Alice was furious. I immediately reversed course and went back to the Needham Dump, and in full view of 'townies' I climbed into the huge trash bin and burrowed through yellow bag after yellow bag muttering to St. Anthony. Eventually I returned home, proudly presenting Alice with two Raggedy Ann dolls that looked none the worse for their travels.

"Two?" Alice wailed, "There were three where is the other one?" Back I went — only to find that the town truck came and trash bin was gone. Alice, and Katie, would have rejoice in that two 'Raggedy Ann's, in hand' is better than three Raggedy Ann's in the dumpster. At that point I was feeling a bit raggedy myself. Who was it that said, "No good deed goes unpunished"?

As is generally the case in the Kennedy family, an unaddressed disturbance ferments animosity, an addressed disturbance imbues tranquility. Yes, two out of three, not a bad batting average, restored peace and quiet to the family domicile. Father Dan was truly the most relieved because his initiative to clean out his room per-petrated the crisis.

That night while dining out with priest friends, who knew us well, Father Dan had them hooting at the image of his old man gamely climbing in and out of trash bins. It was a happy gathering, celebrating Father Dan's new assignment and Bill Lohan's upcom-ing ordination as a transitional deacon. Father Matt Westcott and Father Bob Blaney completed the gang.

During dinner Father Dan startled everyone by making an odd proposal, that each of them take out a life insurance policy on each other. He was not joking as he was wont to do, he was definitely serious. Father Dan went on to point out that, statistically, one of them would die young; so why not at least have a few dollars with which to commiserate? Of course his suggestion was roundly ridiculed as morbid and preposterous. Only in retrospect did his friends wonder what inspired him to make such a suggestion.

On Saturday morning before he returned to St. John the Evan-gelist for his last weekend, he sat at our computer with me as I listened to the Irish Music radio program. When the DJ played 'Danny Boy' he turned to me and said; "That's a great song, isn't it Dad?" I responded, "Yes, it is; did you enjoy hearing it sung at your Ordination Reception?" As was his habit, he rapidly spun his head around to face me and said, "Did you have something to do with that?" I replied, "Yes, I pre-arranged with Andy Healey, the band leader, to start playing 'Danny Boy' after I introduced you." He looked at me, said nothing and then rapidly spun his head back to the computer. I was disappointed that he did not comment as to whether or not he liked the introduction. After he died we came across a picture of him laughing raucously as I was introducing him so I have subsequently concluded that even though he didn't voice his sentiments he did in fact like the introduction.

Farewell Mass

Rely on the mighty Lord; constantly seek His face. (1 Chronicles 16:11)

On Father Dan's final weekend in Winthrop, he spoke at every Mass in hopes of thanking as many parishioners as possible for their generous welcome to him. He praised them for staying true to the Catholic Church as he said; "the first eight months of my priesthood will always belong to you". His voice began to quiver under the emotional strain of leaving people he truly loved but he summoned the strength to continue as he said; "Remember, as long as there are good and faithful people like, you, God will send happy, healthy, holy priests to serve you," he assured them. Then Father Dan concluded with a personal message;

> *"People come into our lives, and people go out of our lives; priests may be re-assigned from one parish to another parish. One person who will never go out of our lives, who will always remain with us, is Christ. Christ always remains with us! He is the constant in our lives. As you live your lives, keep Christ the constant."*

After his death the St. John the Evangelist Parish Youth Group adopted "Keep Christ the Constant" as their motto, wearing wristbands and tee shirts bearing Father Dan's parting admonition.

Father Patrick Armano was aware that Father Dan was experiencing extreme difficulty in leaving so many good friends at St John the Evangelist Parish and they spoke often of his impending departure. Father Armano said, "Father Dan was truly concerned about leaving the parishioners of St. John the Evangelist behind. In just a few months he developed a deep affection for people he barely knew. I was deeply impressed with the depth of his love. He had the heart of a true shepherd."

Following Father Dan's 'final' Sunday Mass at St. John the Evangelist on January 27, 2008, a Farewell Reception was held in the Religious Education Building. Students had made posters saying, Goodbye Father Dan, God Bless You Father Dan, Thank You Father Dan and, Come Back and See Us, Father Dan! Personal and emotional messages were also inscribed on the various posters. Father Dan shook hands with and embraced the dozens of parishioners who lined up to say farewell. Many asked for his priestly blessing.

As the recipient of warm words of thanks he was pleased but also embarrassed. Although he had only been at St. John the Evangelist for a short time he had obviously 'connected' with many parishioners. His gratitude shown in his eyes as people mentioned specific actions undertaken, words thoughtfully spoken, and being a model for the youth of the parish; a "faith-filled, fun loving, normal guy." Several young people said they would miss his Trivia Nights; they loved his ability to mix hearty laughter with deep respect for the Catholic faith and his clear love of the Eucharist.

As the crowd thinned, Father Dan made his apologies and dashed away to another engagement. Months earlier he had promised to perform a baptism for friends in Connecticut on the afternoon of January 27th. Once the time of the Farewell Reception was announced, Father Dan advised Matt and Erin Blute that he might be running late, but they could count on him to welcome their baby, Kelly Elizabeth, as the newest member of the Catholic Church. Father Dan tossed his gear in his car and took off, bound for Fairfield, CT a three-hour drive from Winthrop, MA.

Father Dan made good time on his trek to Fairfield, CT and Kelly's baptism went smoothly. It had been a hectic day, an emotional day, a high-octane day – Father Dan's kind of day! He considered it the utmost of blessings to be asked to minister to his friends and their children. Father Dan loved to celebrate Nuptial Masses, witnessing men and women, whom he loved, pledge their fidelity to God and to one another. One of his most favorite privileges as a priest was administering the Sacrament of Baptism. He truly loved baptisms; to Father Dan, the mind-boggling miracle of a soul becoming a child of Christ, a member of the Catholic Church for perpetuity was an overwhelming manifestation of the God's love for His people.

Kelly Elizabeth's welcome into the Catholic Church and Father Dan's blessing of her parents and godparents was a joyous occasion for him. Unbeknown to anyone at time, this would be his last ministerial function.

Fr. Dan Kennedy with newly baptized Kelly Elizabeth Blute.

Chapter 16: We Need Men Who Think Like You

"Come follow me..." (Matthew 4:19)

Catholicism is Winning

"You God are my King from of old, winning victories throughout the earth."
(Psalm 74:12)

All his life Danny and I had long-standing jokes, like his bone-crushing handshake, that he never seemed to tire of. One started when he was about eight and supposedly tucked in bed. I was watching the Red Sox on television when he appeared, asking sleepily, "Who's winning?" I was irked that he was still up and growled unhelpfully, "3 to 1. Now get back to bed."

Of course he persisted, "No, who's winning? I want to know." But I would not give in, repeating "3 to 1." After a few back-and-forth's, I finally relented and let him watch a few innings before sending him back upstairs, but the joke took on a life of its own. As an adult when he would be on a business trip the phone would ring and as I answered, he uttered sometimes loudly, sometimes inaudibly, "Who's winning?"

One night it was a long-distance call from Kuala Lumpur, Malaysia, where Dan was on a trip for Cabot Corporation. The phone rang and I heard a demanding; "Who's winning?" as he shouted into the phone. I responded in a 'matter of fact' subdued tone; "14 to 7." "I didn't call from half-way around the world for the score," Dan roared. "I want to know: Who's winning?"

At that point our sparing was over and I broke the good news: The New England Patriots were in fact leading the Indianapolis Colts 14 to 7. We were both laughing. I loved playing that stupid game with Dan — and there was no way he could crush my hand from halfway around the world. Boy, I sure miss his joking ways.

Our old joke sprang to mind in 2012 when I noticed an article in the Wall Street Journal called "Traditional Catholicism Is Winning." The authors, Anne Hendershott and Christopher White, described the steady rise in seminary enrollments and religious vocations nationally, and quoted Pope Benedict XVI's insight that "true renewal" of the Church can be seen in a more widespread "joy of faith." The photo illustration accompanying the article depicted Cardinal Seán O'Malley at the Cathedral of the Holy Cross ordaining Daniel J. Kennedy, to the Holy Priesthood in 2007. The picture, which currently is displayed on our living room wall, does not mention of him by name but it is, undeniably, newly ordained, Father Daniel J. Kennedy.

That same year, 2012, Bishop Emeritus John McCarthy of the Diocese of Austin, Texas, posted on his blog an article, "The Clergy Should Laugh More," illustrated by a photo of a laughing priest — Father Dan Kennedy. Since Father Dan's death more people have requested copies of Father Dan's 'laughing picture' than any other.

As Father Dan's parishioners at Winthrop and Scituate often told him, it's a great delight to know a priest who exudes happiness. Father Dan was both a happy priest and one who loved to laugh. Certainly part of Father Dan's appeal to young Catholics was his ability to joke and to see joy in life. He did not pretend life is always a bed of roses, but he showed that friendship, laughter and love are divine gifts we should relish and share generously with everyone we meet. *"Cheerfulness strengthens the heart and makes us persevere in a good life. Therefore the Servant of God ought to always be in good spirits." (Saint Philip Neri)*

Even after Father Dan died he was springing jokes. One had roots in his ordination, when his niece Ashley pretended disgust at all the photographs taken of him. What vanity! How unspiritual! Father Dan pretended to ignore her teasing; he was already plotting a retort. On Christmas Day when Ashley un-wrapped her gift from Uncle Danny she found a golf ball box relabeled: "More Pictures of Danny." Ashley was indignant. As she proceeded to open the box detected a sly smile slowly creep across Danny's face as he knew she was anticipating a box full of pictures.

Ashley was relieved and thrilled to discover that the altered golf ball box actually contained a carefully chosen piece of jewelry. Ashley was happy, Danny was happy and everyone had a good laugh at the 'Christmas Picture Ploy'. To the subsequent surprise of the entire family, that was not the end of the picture ploy.

For many years Danny and Ashley had a ritual of putting up the Manger scene together. This was Danny's way of sharing his love of the Nativity with his young niece. After Epiphany, while packing it away together, the two would hide the Baby Jesus figure in a secret place however, in January 2008 Danny managed to place Baby Jesus in his 'secret hiding place'; secretly.

Shortly before Christmas Eve in 2008, our first Christmas without Danny, Ashley set up the Manger by herself; on Christmas morning when she went to take Baby Jesus out of the 'secret hiding place' she discovered that Baby Jesus was wrapped in a picture; a picture of Danny! Immediately all of us knew Danny's spirit was with us laughing raucously at Ashley's shock as she saw his picture. This was not at all how he had planned his prank to develop, but it is exactly how God willed it to develop. As usual, Father knows best!

In Ashley's mind, Danny's memory will never dim. "He was wonderful," she said. "Even though his journey as a priest was short-lived, much too short, that's why it stands out. The thing is, no matter how long he lived he would have been a fireball — that's just the way he rolled." She added, "The soul, the spirit, and love are timeless, and they remain even when the body fails. Still, it's sad to lose a guy who ultimately was the coolest priest you'd ever want to meet."

Stop, Look, and Listen

Ask the master of the harvest to send out laborers for his harvest." (Luke 10:2b)

Father Joseph Barranger, Prior of the Dominican House of Studies in Washington, DC, knew Father Dan well, having mentored him at Providence College and, after graduation, he became his Spiritual Director. "He was an enthusiastic cheerleader for vocations; in eight short months he had a tremendous impact on a number of people, especially the young," Father Barranger recalled. "I trust completely in God's Providence and I know that the work God did through Father Dan's priesthood is not limited by time and space. I believe that his short priesthood on earth has eternal consequences both for himself and for a great many other people."

Father Dan's influence has even survived his death. Often friends have confided with Alice and me that recollections of him seem to occur unexpectedly. One of these instances occurred four years after Father Dan went home to the Lord.

In 2012, a high school and a college classmate of mine, Paul Kane, a resident of northern Vermont, whom I had not seen in over fifty years, unexpectedly, sent me a note in which he described attending a Saturday afternoon Mass in St. Johnsbury, Vermont. In his homily the celebrant related the Gospel's message of faith to a Funeral Mass he attended for a young priest from the Archdiocese of Boston. The priest went on to say; "although that young priest's life on earth was abbreviated, his short life as a priest and, his family's trust in God's plan, were examples of faith in action and were underscored by the families appeal for continual prayers from the laity for priestly vocations."

Although the Vermont priest did not identify the 'young priest from Boston' Paul was motivated to speak with him after Mass to learn identity of the Boston priest. Paul's conjecture was affirmed; the deceased priest was, Father Dan Kennedy.

In 2008, Father William T. Schmidt, Pastor of St. Patrick's Church in Stoneham, MA wrote a commemorative book on the Bicentennial of the Archdiocese of Boston. His book; 'Two Hundred Years of Catholic Priesthood in Boston' cited two young priests who died after brief ministries, Father Patrick J. Power and Father Joseph E. Laporte. Father Schmidt recalled that; "many miracles have occurred at Father Power's gravesite in Holy Cross Cemetery in Malden, MA and Father Laporte left a remarkable legacy as the 'Don Bosco of Southie'. He added; "Today we are left to wonder whether the same charisma would have blessed the same neighborhoods in South Boston through the ministry of Father Dan Kennedy. As Father Dan's driving passion was the promotion of vocations to the priesthood, perhaps the miracles of Father Power will be paralleled in years ahead by an increase in priestly vocations attributed to the example and the intercession of Father Dan Kennedy."

When I began to write this book my intention was to document Father Dan's life for future family generations. As that project progressed it seemed to gravitate toward a "help wanted" ad for vocations to priesthood. That's even better! I hope everyone who reads this book will encourage young men to pray fervently and to ask the Lord to speak to their souls; perhaps in a loud voice.

After all, each of us has a vocation, but only a chosen few are called to bring us Christ Himself, truly present, in the Eucharist, to the people of God in the seven Sacraments. I am grateful for every man who has answered God's call, at great personal sacrifice, to share the Joy of Christ with His people. The Catholic Church is winning when happy, healthy, holy men hear, answer, and run the race that Father Dan ran — consumed with the Joy of the Lord, radiating His Love and, thrilled beyond words to serve at the Altar of Our Lord and Savior, Jesus Christ.

I have competed well; I have finished the race; I have kept the faith. (2 Timothy 4:7)

Every day I thank God for calling our son to His Holy Priesthood, and I also thank Him for calling Father Dan to Altar of the Lord where Alice and I hope to see him again, at the Eternal Banquet.

Thank you Lord for providing Holy Priests to tend Your Flock!

APPENDIX

Words of Remembrance

Church of St. Joseph, Needham, February 1, 2008

Reverend Daniel J. Kennedy

Born: January 16, 1974
Ordained: May 26, 2007
Eternal Life: January 27, 2008

On behalf of our family, I would like to thank Cardinal Seán, Bishop Hennessey, Father Westcott, Father Armano, and Monsignor McGann. I would also like to thank everyone at St. John the Evangelist in Winthrop who have helped him, Father Bourke and especially Joe Mazzone who will be ordained to the diaconate to-morrow. I also want to thank everyone who has been so kind to us in the past few days.

Many have asked; "What can we do to help you?" I have a suggestion for your consideration on what could be done to help our family. Please pray for vocations to the priesthood. Every morning when you rise from bed offer your entire day for an increase in vocations to the priesthood. Thank you!

Shortly before his Ordination, while Danny was having breakfast with me here in Needham, he looked me straight in the eye and with great 'conviction' said; "Dad, I intend to be GOOD at this"... and, he was!

I am also reminded of a story that I wanted to relate at his Ordination Reception but did not because I didn't want to incur his ire. As you may well know, he was not reticent in expressing consternation and I feared for my life if I had told this story. As the Lord said; "Be hot or be cold but don't be lukewarm." I don't think anyone would ever accuse Father Dan of being lukewarm! Now, I can tell the story with fear of reprisal.

Many years ago when he was 7 years old, he played an exceptional hockey game at the Fitzpatrick Hockey Rink in Holyoke against a team from South Hadley. He scored (6) goals in that game; quite an accomplishment for a young boy. On the way home that night when we were driving past the old Westfield Sanitarium on East Mountain Road he looked up at the stars in the sky and said, "I wonder what God is doing tonight?" I was shocked by that remark as most young kids would have been thinking about the (6) goals, the pinnacle of a young life, yet he wanted to know 'what God was doing tonight'. I really don't remember what I said, probably, "God must be pleased that you scored (6) goals." (Actually, he could have scored more goals if he didn't spend so much time in the penalty box).

Now, 'he' knows what God is doing tonight!

Shortly after he arrived at St. John the Evangelist he was called to the hospital to anoint a dying woman. The woman asked him if 'he' knew what Heaven was like. He told her that he had no idea what Heaven was like. Then he added, "In a few days, 'you' will know what Heaven is like and the rest of us will still be down here scratching our 'heads'. In his own unique way he was able to offer her, hope of Heaven. After he left the hospital the dying woman told her daughter that she wanted that young priest to say her Funeral Mass. A few days later a call came to the Rectory requesting that Father Kennedy say the Funeral Mass for the woman. That staff at the Rectory queried him and said, "You just arrived in Winthrop and already people are requesting 'you' to say Funeral Masses?"

Now, 'he' knows.....what Heaven is like...and the rest of us are still down here scratching 'our' heads.

I have been fearful that this day would occur; for me it is not totally unanticipated. In at least three consecutive generations in the history of our Kennedy Clan, parents have been asked to return a son to the Lord. This marks the 4th generation. Consequently, for some time, I have been prepared to cite a verse which I believe is appropriate and I hope that I can proclaim it with 'conviction'.

"THE LORD GIVETH AND THE LORD TAKETH AWAY....BLESS-ED BE THE NAME OF THE LORD."

In the name of the Father and of the Son and the Holy Spirit. Amen.

- Daniel J. Kennedy, Sr.

The Boston Pilot Newspaper: Meet our seminarians: Daniel J. Kennedy Jr.

Posted: 12/8/2006

This week The Pilot, in cooperation with the Office of Vocations, begins a series of brief profiles of the men preparing for the priesthood in the Archdiocese of Boston.

Home Parish: St. Joseph Needham

Seminary: St. John's Seminary

High-School: Catholic Memorial High School

College: Providence College

Hobbies: Running, Golf, Red Sox, NE Pats

When was the first time you thought of priesthood?

I thought of it as a child, thanks to the fine priests who came through St. Mary's in Westfield, MA and St. Joseph's in Needham. However it did not seriously enter into my head until after college.

What were major Catholic activities you participated in prior to the Seminary?

I attended the vocations retreat for the archdiocese in 1999. It was quite helpful to finally take a concrete step toward investigating God's call in my life. The retreat helped me understand that I was a few years from being ready to make the jump into the seminary formation program.

What is your favorite Scripture passage? Why?

Psalm 46 "Be still and know that I am God". In today's busy world, so many of us are constantly looking for the quick and clean answer to so many questions in life. Sometimes it is helpful to just stop and reflect upon the Creator, and then trust in His plan for each of us.

Who influenced/inspired you to priesthood? Please explain.

A handful of parish priests, the Irish Christian Brothers at Catholic Memorial and the Dominican Friars at Providence College. These men were among the happiest I have ever encountered.

What would people be surprised to know about you?

I am training for my 9th marathon in the last 6 years.

Did anybody invite you to consider priesthood?

The nuns I had in elementary school asked my classmates and me regularly if we had ever considered priesthood. As well as, Bishop Joseph Maguire, Father Francis Reilly, Msgr. Jim Haddad, Father Joseph Barranger, Mrs. Mary MacGillicuddy.

How did you come to know Jesus Christ?

Through the example my parents provided for me as a child. Their word and action demonstrated a deep faith in Jesus Christ.

What were the spiritual events or activities that helped you develop and shape your personal relationship with Christ and His Church?

Attending Mass, going to confession and spending time before the Blessed Sacrament in Eucharistic Adoration.

What signs led you to believe that God was calling you to be a priest?

I had a great job, great pay, great travel opportunities, I had unbelievable place in the Charlestown Navy Yard and a terrific girlfriend. With all that the fact that the priesthood was rattling around in my head gave me pause. As I took steps to investigate this notion, God began to make it more and more clear to me.

Through the Cardinal, God is calling you personally to help rebuild his Church. How must the priest respond to this mandate today?

Our Church right now needs normal, everyday men to muster the courage to respond, "Here I am Lord". So many Catholics do not attend Mass for a number of reasons. We need to re-educate Catholics as to the relevance of a faith life and the practice of that faith on a regular basis. A priest needs to remain connected to mainstream everyday life, while at the same time he needs to be different. Much the same way as a parent needs to be in tune with all that their children say and do, while at the same time holding themselves apart, not necessarily above, but apart, if we hope to be the compass or the rudder for people as they navigate through the waters of life.

CardinalSeansBlog.org: The reflections of a newly ordained priest

Hello and welcome all to my blog!

As I mentioned in my last posting, I thought these first two weeks of July would be a wonderful opportunity for some of our newly ordained priests to share their reflections on the time since their ordinations in May. This week, I am pleased to bring you a guest posting by Father Daniel Kennedy who, along with six other fine men, I ordained to the priesthood on May 26. In June, he began his assignment as parochial vicar at St. John the Evangelist Parish in Winthrop.

I wish to express my thanks to Father Kennedy for his willingness to put this post together even in the midst of a very busy holiday week.

I hope you enjoy this guest post and may you all have a blessed and safe summer!

+ Cardinal Seán

* * *

As I reflect upon my first six weeks as a priest, there are a full range of notions and emotions which come to mind. Each day seems to be a new adventure. Both the ordinary and the extraordinary have taken on a new meaning as I adjust to the new configuration of my identity.

The Ordination and Mass of thanksgiving over Memorial Day weekend were milestones in my life, unlike any other. The sight of the Cathedral of the Holy Cross teeming with people who truly love the priesthood should be in every vocations video.

The sheer joy on the faces of so many in attendance will be with me forever. What a great day for Christ's Church. On a personal level, I was so moved by the opportunity to share such a special weekend with so many family and friends, who through prayers, encouragement and patience helped make the realization of my vocation a reality. My 13-year-old niece told me that she never thought she would have to wait in line to talk with her uncle.

* * *

My first Mass at my home parish of St. Joseph in Needham was in many ways a dream come true. I had been to a few first Masses at St. Joseph's years ago, but the fact that this one was in thanksgiving for the priesthood that the Lord has asked me to share, really blew me away.

I was surrounded by priests who had been instrumental in my formation and development over the years. With me at the altar were Fathers Francis Reilly, Charles Higgins, Michael Lawlor and Brian Manning. The bookends were Father Francis Kennedy who baptized me 33 years ago and Father Brian Manning, my deacon intern supervisor who taught me so much about priesthood. In between were many happy, holy and healthy priests who have provided an invaluable priestly witness along the way. My dear friend and ever so patient mentor, Father Charlie Higgins preached the homily. The altar servers were young men that I have known and watched grow since the day they were born.

My sisters Katie and Anne Marie and my brother Jack proudly and eloquently proclaimed the word of God. My sister Patti, my niece Ashley and my aunt Judy presented the gifts and my dear parents presented me with a most beautiful chalice in memory of the Kennedy and Haggerty families.

I knew when I entered formation that going it alone was not a possibility. The first Mass of thanksgiving was such a great way to celebrate with those who kept me focused, kept me sane and made me feel so loved along the way.

I do not believe that there is any class or course of study which could fully prepare one for the enormity and awesome nature of Holy Orders. My first few days at St. John the Evangelist in Winthrop, simply put, have been in many ways like beginning a new job, that is, a new job which will last forever, a vocation I was born to fulfill. Everywhere I turn there has been a new face, a new experience, a new system with which one needs to become familiar.

I began my first weekend by speaking after Communion at each Mass, as a way to introduce myself to the faithful of the parish.

I explained that although we do not know each other well, from what I have already learned of this great community, I feel that right off the bat, there are some things we all share in common: a love for God, a love for family and a passion for all things that are the Boston Red Sox. I explained that I am a priest so anxious to serve this parish, as well as a left fielder looking for a softball team!

Celebrating Mass everyday is about as humbling an experience as I have had in my life. Truth be told, a great deal of energy is spent ensuring that I am celebrating the Mass properly. I have been told to loosen up a little bit. I think I know what that means, but it may take a while. I was reminded of a prayer to be said before Mass and I have found it particularly meaningful. "Lord may I celebrate this Eucharist in union with you, as though it were my first Eucharist, my only Eucharist, my last Eucharist." It is my hope that I will never lose sight of the privilege it is to bring Christ, truly present in the Eucharist, to the good people of God.

In addition to saying Mass, I have had the opportunity to celebrate the sacraments of Baptism, Penance and Anointing of the Sick. Each ministerial encounter has been unique. Comforting is the fact that the sacraments actually do something, they are true encounters with Christ. I call upon myself to decrease, while Christ increases.

Clear to me in such a short period of time as a priest has been the fact that Catholics truly crave Christ in the Eucharist. There is such a desire to come to know Christ more and more each day through His Word, and to be nourished by Him who is the Bread of Life.

I have also been touched by how welcoming, helpful, and forgiving of my rookie mistakes people have been. Such support fills me with a great deal of hope for the priesthood in which I share.

Fr. Daniel Kennedy

http://www.cardinalseansblog.org/2007/07/06/the-reflections-of-a-newly-ordained-priest/

Obituary: Father Daniel Kennedy, one of archdiocese's newest priests

The Boston Pilot Newspaper

By Father Robert M. O'Grady

Posted: 2/8/2008

A priest who had been ordained by Cardinal Seán P. O'Malley just seven months ago, Father Daniel J. Kennedy died suddenly at St. Francis Hospital in Hartford, Conn. on Jan. 27. He had just celebrated his 34th birthday three weeks prior, on Jan. 6.

Father Kennedy was born in Holyoke one of the five children of Daniel and Alice (Haggarty) Kennedy. The family moved to Needham where he attended St. Joseph Parish School and West Roxbury's Catholic Memorial High School. He subsequently graduated from Providence College and worked for a time at Cabot Corporation in Billerica.

His mother said that she thought that the "idea of the priest-hood was in his mind since he was a young boy." He delayed the answer to the call, but eventually he entered St. John's Seminary in preparation for ordination. An accomplished athlete who took excellent care of his physical health -- he was a familiar figure jogging the hills of the seminary grounds and streets of Brighton. He had participated in several marathons and was preparing for another. His father noted he was a great athlete and favored hockey over all sports. He quipped "if he'd spent less time in the penalty box, he'd have scored more goals."

Father Kennedy was also a reserve chaplain in the United States Navy and had recently served a few weeks on the USS Nimitz. Among his several passions was promoting vocations to the priesthood. Whether celebrating Mass, shooting hoops with young parishioners in Winthrop or prepping for a marathon, he always wanted to be a model for those young men considering the priesthood. Prior to ordination he had spent his deacon year at St. Mary of the Nativity Parish, Scituate.

Father Kennedy's funeral Mass was celebrated at St. Joseph Church, Needham on Feb. 1. It was at that same altar just seven months before that he had celebrated his first Mass following ordination. The celebrant of the funeral Mass was Cardinal O'Malley who was moved to tears several times during the Mass.

The homilist was Central Regional Bishop Robert Hennessey, who had once been assigned at St. Joseph Parish, serving there when Father Kennedy was a youngster. Bishop Hennessey admitted that this was "one of the most difficult things he had to do as a priest or bishop." Preaching to some 200 priests, including classmates, seminary contemporaries and many friends and brother priests; to a church filled with people crowding the aisles, and especially to the family, the bishop began by saying "We have not come to celebrate a life, but to mourn a death." This was certainly a funeral that, while filled with hope, was overwhelmingly sad.

Before the Final Commendation, Father Kennedy's father, Dan, spoke and told those assembled that he had been asked over the course of the days since his son's death "What can we do for you?" He answered "Pray for vocations to the priesthood. Dan loved being a priest and he wanted others to consider it seriously. For him and for us -- pray for vocations."

In addition to his parents, Father Kennedy's survivors are his sisters, Kathleen, Patricia and Anne Marie, all of Needham and a brother John, Simsbury Conn. Father Kennedy was buried in St. Mary Cemetery, Westfield on Feb. 2. Attending the Commendation rites were Springfield's Bishop Timothy McDonnell and former Bishop Joseph Maguire.

As readers note there are two obituaries for archdiocesan priests this week. They will further see that these two priests: Father Walter Stocklosa and Father Daniel Kennedy were the "bookends of the presbyterate" -- Father Stocklosa the longest ordained at almost 68 years, and Father Kennedy among the most recent, at about seven months.

Each served this archdiocese with zeal and joy, each loved being a priest; each leaves many people: family, friends, folks young and old who received something of Jesus Christ from each of these priests' ministry.

For Father Stocklosa we can adjust Bishop Hennessey's words and truly say, "We have come to celebrate a life as well as to mourn a death." With him we mourn Father Kennedy's death. For both we say to God, and their respective families "thank you for their faithful priestly lives."

CardinalSeansBlog.org: Comments on Father Kennedy's sudden death

This week it was quite a shock for all of us that a young priest ordained last May, Father Daniel Kennedy, died suddenly of a heart attack in his brother's home.

I had seen Father Dan recently, and I asked him, "How are things going?" He replied, "Cardinal, it's wonderful to be a priest." I could see how enthusiastic he was. He had been working in the chaplaincy program with the Navy, and he was very engaged with his parish ministry. He also wrote on this blog last summer of his experience as he was just beginning his ministry.

Because he was a young man who was apparently so healthy and who had participated many times in the Boston Marathon, of course there was no warning of his imminent death. As a result, the surprise and grief at his passing was very, very great.

Our sympathy goes out to his parents and family. Dan was very close to his family — a beautiful family.

As today was his funeral Mass, we ask people to pray for him and pray for his family. We also pray that other young men will be inspired by his generosity and enthusiasm for the priesthood. Although his ministry here was short, we know that he is a priest forever.

http://www.cardinalseansblog.org/2008/02/01/

Pastor's Corner

Father Ken Cannon, St. Mary of the Nativity

On September 21st, we will be having our 16th annual golf tournament, which was renamed in 2008 to St. Mary of the Nativity Fr. Daniel J. Kennedy Memorial Golf Tournament. This tournament raises money for both the parish and a scholarship fund in Fr. Kennedy's name for a seminarian in need at St. John's Seminary in Brighton.

For those new to the parish, Fr. Dan Kennedy spent three years here in Scituate during his time in the seminary. He touched the lives of both young and old and everyone in between with his faith, youth and vitality. One of the things he did here was teach religious education to our students leaving a lasting impression with many of them. For several years Daniel was one of the most popular Confirmation names chosen by the young men making their Confirmation.

Fr. Kennedy was ordained a priest in the spring of 2007 and was assigned to St. John the Evangelist Parish in Winthrop where he shared his faith and love of the Church with that community. On January 27, 2008 he completed his assignment there and was getting ready for his new assignment at Gate of Heaven Parish in South Boston. Later that day, while visiting his brother in Connecticut, Fr. Kennedy died of a heart attack due to an undiagnosed congenital heart defect. This came as a shock to all who knew him because he was a marathon runner and he was only thirty- four years old.

To show their love and appreciation for Fr. Dan the parish changed the name of our golf tournament to honor him and contribute to the scholarship fund established in his name. If you play golf and you would like to support this worthy cause you can still sign up to play. If you do not play golf but would like to participate in this event you may attend the dinner at Hatherly Country Club or you could volunteer to help at the course. Please call the parish office Monday morning.

Sincerely yours in Christ,

Fr. Cannon

Father (Lt.) Daniel J. Kennedy, USN Memorial Bridge

On June 15, 2015, the Feast Day of St. Alice, the Commonwealth of Massachusetts dedicated a bridge over Interstate Route 95 in Needham, Massachusetts, in honor of Father (Lt.) Daniel J. Kennedy. Father Dan is memorialized by a plaque embedded in the bridge which reads as follows:

Humbled to be a priest, a happy priest. He radiated joy, taught with vigor and conviction, ran nine marathons, and was a proud member of the Knights of Columbus. Father Dan grew up in Needham, attended St. Joseph's School, Catholic Memorial High School, Providence College, and St. John's Seminary. He served as a Chaplain on the USS Nimitz CVN-68, and passionately promoted vocations to the priesthood.

"...keep Christ the Constant in your life..."

"...that I may never lose sight of the privilege it is to bring Christ, truly present in the Eucharist, to the good people of God..."

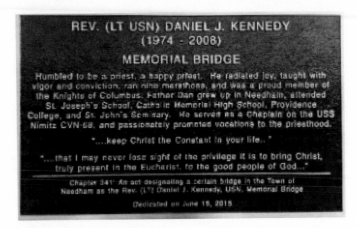

"As a priest, Father Dan was himself a bridge between God and his people. In his ministry, the mercy of Christ and the love of God was revealed to us. We gather today to give thanks to God for the gift of his life and his priesthood."

[Cardinal Seán P. O'Malley]

"A bridge is a powerful symbol, and in this case extreme-ly meaningful. I am mindful today of the many times that Danny crossed that bridge in his life. I am mindful thinking of Danny with terms also like 'building bridges.'" [Sen. Michael F. Rush, Danny's great friend who sponsored the bill to dedicate the bridge in Father Kennedy's honor].

"All priests and bishops are called to be pontiffs, bridge builders, and that is what Dan did with his life. Your presence, and the size of this crowd, is testament to that reality. Notice what a bridge is. It remains immovable. It remains still and solid, so that it bridges the gap, so that you may get to where you are going. That is what Christ does. That is what his Holy Church does. That is what Dan did in his priesthood" [Father Matt Westcott, Danny's Ordination Classmate and great friend before blessing the bridge].

"We all miss Danny. We all have fond memories of Danny, and it's days like this that I want you all to know how meaningful it is for our family to celebrate his life in this way" [Jack Kennedy, Danny's brother].

ACKNOWLEDGEMENTS

Dozens of friends, relatives, and perfect strangers have kindly shared their memories of Father Dan. This book would not exist without their contributions; Space does not permit identifying all but I am particularly appreciative for Father Matt Westcott's willingness to contribute to the manuscript as well as his frequent reprimands for my propensity to procrastinate.

It is impossible for me to express the depth of my appreciation to so many of his friends who willingly shared their recollections. Your contributions enabled me to 'show' Father Dan from the prism of many eyes not just from the prejudicial eyes of his father. For everyone who shared their reminiscences' THANK YOU.

Alice and I are extremely grateful to the parishioners of St. Edith Stein Parish in Brockton, St. Mary of the Nativity Parish in Scituate, and St. John the Evangelist Parish in Winthrop, and St. Brigid/Gate of Heaven Parishes in South Boston for the love they displayed and continue to display, for our son.

For their tireless work in assembling and critiquing the manuscript, I want to convey my deep gratitude Marguerite Cail and Ellen Curtin without whom this work would never have materialized.

When this project was not much more than a figment of my imagination, Scot Landry, enthusiastically encouraged me to pursue this goal. I want to thank Scot for his initial reaction of positivity and for his subsequent consultative discussions without which this work would not have been brought to fruition.

I also want to specifically thank Father Dan's good friend, Billy Condron for sharing his personal recollection of Father Dan's extensive discernment stratagem during a most critical point in his life.

Most importantly I want to publically acknowledge my gratitude to the Holy Spirit who in no small way subtly sharpened my recollection faculties in order to include significant spiritual mile markers on Father Dan's tortuous path to priesthood.

Of utmost importance was the tolerance of my family as they dealt with the ebb and flow of my emotions during this ongoing enterprise. Thank you for your patient endurance. I am grateful to my sister Judy, my daughter Katie, my son Jack and my granddaughter Ashley Tara Clare Kennedy for perusing preliminary manuscript drafts. I am also grateful to Patti, Anne Marie and Dave Russell for their constant support in keeping me focused as well as their unwavering efforts to perpetuate Danny's memory.

Finally, even though she was unable to provide current input to the manuscript, I want to thank my lovely wife Alice for being a fabulous mother to our five children and for providing many years of invaluable input for all five of our children. Painstakingly, Alice imparted life's lessons to all of us, especially to her redheaded son the recipient of her genuine interest in, and love for, the people of God. Although it may be a trite expression, it certainly does have application; our union was truly, a marriage made in heaven. Consequently, thank you, Jesus!

Lastly, it is also my hope that, someday, when my younger grandchildren are older; Celia E. and John B. Kennedy, and, Daniel

Francis Russell will read this book and experience the depth of the love their Uncle Danny radiated for his friend, Jesus.

PRAYER FOR PRIESTLY VOCATIONS

Cardinal Seán Patrick O'Malley, O.F.M. Cap.

Archdiocese of Boston

Holy Mother of the Good Shepherd,

turn your motherly care to our Archdiocese.

Intercede for us to the Lord of the Harvest

to send more laborers to the harvest.

Inspire vocations in our time.

Let the word of your Son be made flesh

anew in the lives of persons anxious to proclaim

the Good News of everlasting life.

Draw them near to the heart of your Son

so that they can understand the beauty and the joy

that awaits them to be His witnesses. Amen.

PROCEEDS & BOOK WEBSITE

All net proceeds from this book will be donated to the

Father Daniel J. Kennedy Memorial Scholarship Fund

at Saint John's Seminary in Brighton, MA.

Additional photos, multimedia and links are available

on the book's website: www.247days.org.